SAP® NetWeaver BI 7.0 Migration Guide

SAP® Essentials

Expert SAP knowledge for your day-to-day work

Whether you wish to expand your SAP knowledge, deepen it, or master a use case, SAP Essentials provide you with targeted expert knowledge that helps support you in your day-to-day work. To the point, detailed, and ready to use.

SAP PRESS is a joint initiative of SAP and Galileo Press. The know-how offered by SAP specialists combined with the expertise of the Galileo Press publishing house offers the reader expert books in the field. SAP PRESS features first-hand information and expert advice, and provides useful skills for professional decision-making.

SAP PRESS offers a variety of books on technical and business related topics for the SAP user. For further information, please visit our website:
www.sap-press.com.

Egger, Fiechter, Kramer, Sawicki, Weber
SAP Business Intelligence (BI)
2007, 656 pp., ISBN 978-1-59229-082-6

Galoppin, Caems
Managing Organizational Change during SAP Implementations
2007, 364 pp., ISBN 978-1-59229-104-5

Vanstechelman, Mergaerts, Matthys
SAP NetWeaver Application Server Upgrade Guide
2007, 582 pp., ISBN 978-1-59229-144-1

Scholer, Zink
SAP Governance, Risk and Compliance
2008, 380 pp., ISBN 978-1-59229-191-5

Daniel Knapp

SAP® NetWeaver BI 7.0 Migration Guide

Galileo Press

Bonn • Boston

Contents

Introduction

The term "migration," which derives from the Latin *migratio* (to ramble or hike), describes a simple concept. However, many companies associate a time-consuming and complex process with it. Usually, companies are faced with the topic of migration when new software releases are available or the maintenance period of the product that's currently being used expires. With regard to the data warehousing solution, the latest version of SAP NetWeaver 7.0 Business Intelligence (BI) has been available for two years now; however, approximately 70% of all companies using SAP NetWeaver BI still use one of its predecessors, such as SAP Business Warehouse (BW) 3.x.

One of the many reasons for this may be rooted in an aversion to using new versions that might contain bugs or malfunctions. A similar behavior can be found in the automotive industry: You usually don't buy a new car immediately after it has been introduced to the market. What is even more important is the IT maxim never to touch a running system. This principle indicates that IT systems that work well should not be replaced by other systems whose proper functionality is still uncertain. Not only does this principle apply to complex system landscapes but it also holds true for the operating system of your work center, for example. Would you format the hard disk of your machine and install a new operating system when the old one runs without any problem?

A migration to SAP NetWeaver BI differs from the migration of other systems in several aspects. For example, SAP NetWeaver BI still supports all concepts of SAP BW 3.x, which means you don't need to customize anything. After migrating to SAP NetWeaver BI, you can decide whether you want to customize the system according to the newly available functions, and if so, you can determine when and in what order you want to proceed. The concept migration, that is, the use of new concepts and options, can be carried out in separate steps; a "big bang" implementation isn't necessary.

This book will describe the complete migration from SAP BW 3.x to SAP NetWeaver BI to help you overcome any skepticism related to this migration task. The book starts with a general overview of the topic of migration, followed by a comprehensive description of the technical and the concept migration of SAP NetWeaver BI. After that, the individual areas of a concept migration are covered in greater detail, such as the migration of authorizations and data flows as well as the migration in the context of web reporting. These chapters contain useful real-life examples and cost estimates.

Contents of This Book

To carry out a migration from SAP BW 3.x to SAP NetWeaver BI, you must understand the different concepts of these two releases so that you can migrate them from the legacy system to the new one later. For this reason, each of these concepts is described *in great detail*, which makes the book attractive even for beginners with a basic knowledge of data warehousing solutions as well as the terminology used in this context. However, even the technically savvy users among you should read the introductory Sections 4.1, Data Flow Concepts; 5.1, Authorization Concepts; and 6.1, Concepts Used in Reporting, because performing the migration project requires profound knowledge of the differences between individual concepts.

The book has been written in such a way that you don't have to read it from cover to cover; you can pick those chapters that interest you most. If you don't have any knowledge of migration in general, start with Chapter 3, Concept Migration. To migrate individual areas, you can read the respective chapters only. However, even if you do have sufficient knowledge related to migration, you should read Chapter 3 because it describes the various aspects related to migrating concepts to SAP NetWeaver BI. If you need further information about the technical aspects of a migration, read Chapter 2, Technical Migration.

The book is structured as follows:

- **Chapter 1: Basic Principles of Migration**
  Chapter 1 describes the basic principles of a migration process, including what migration means and why it's necessary. In addition, you'll get an overview of the maintenance cycles for SAP software and of the new functions provided by SAP NetWeaver BI. The chapter ends with a brief outline of potential costs and a summary of the different version names of the SAP data warehousing solution.
- **Chapter 2: Technical Migration**
  Chapter 2 introduces the technical aspects of a migration project as well as its procedures. The chapter describes the objects involved in a technical migration

and the concepts and methods based on which the migration projects are carried out in real life.

- **Chapter 3: Concept Migration**
  The concept migration deals with readjusting concepts from legacy systems. The chapter begins with a description of the concepts available in SAP NetWeaver BI and their objects. After that, the chapter describes the basic principles and processes of the concept migration of these objects, which have been established in practice.
- **Chapter 4: Migrating the Data Flow**
  Chapter 4 provides details on migrating the data flow. In this context, it's important for you to understand the data flow concepts of SAP BW and SAP NetWeaver BI, which are described in detail at the beginning of the chapter. The chapter then continues with a description of the migration concept, that is, how objects of the old data flow are migrated into the new one. After describing the migration concept, we walk through a simple and a complex migration project to show you the possible pitfalls. Chapter 4 ends with real-life observations and a cost estimate.
- **Chapter 5: Migrating Authorizations**
  Chapter 5 provides a detailed description of how to migrate the authorization concept. Similar to Chapter 4, this chapter first describes the two authorization concepts: the legacy system and the new system. After that, the chapter describes the method recommended by SAP for migrating authorizations on the basis of an example. This chapter also closes with real-life observations and an estimate of the costs involved.
- **Chapter 6: Migration in Reporting**
  Migration in the context of web reporting, that is, the migration of queries and reports, is usually a very complex task. Similar to the two preceding chapters, the different concepts used in reporting are introduced at the beginning of Chapter 6, with a special focus on the differences. In reporting, migration projects consist of automatic and manual migration tasks, which are described in greater detail in the course of this chapter. After that, you'll see a query and a web template migrated in a sample project. Because some important web reporting concepts have been eliminated, these aspects are described in great detail along with some recommendations as to how you should proceed in this context. The chapter ends with a reference to real-life scenarios and an estimate of the costs involved.

- **Appendix**
  The Appendices contain useful references to the literature used in this book as well as further reading, a list of abbreviations used, a glossary containing the most important terms from SAP BW and SAP NetWeaver BI, and a comparison of old and new web items available in BEx Web Application Designer.

Target Groups

If you're a part of any of the following groups, the information on migration in this book will be very helpful:

- *Developers* who work in the business intelligence environment and are currently challenged with a migration from SAP BW 3.5 to SAP NetWeaver BI will find valuable information, recommended actions, and comprehensive examples to support their migration tasks.
- *Consultants* who work in the area of business intelligence and have to carry out migration projects from SAP BW 3.5 to SAP NetWeaver BI for customers will find useful practical tips and learn how to have a successful migration.
- *Administrators* and *SAP Basis consultants* who carry out the technical migration and attend the concept migration will obtain an overview of the tasks to be carried out as well as a collection of SAP Notes that leads to the successful migration of legacy systems.
- *Users with a general interest in the topic of migration, students*, and *other users* requiring comprehensive information about the concepts available in SAP BW 3.5 or SAP NetWeaver BI will find detailed descriptions of both old and new concepts in Section 4.1, Data Flow Concepts; Section 5.1, Authorization Concepts; and Section 6.1, Concepts Used in Reporting.

1 Basic Principles of Migration

Migration is a recurring issue in companies. Depending on the size of an enterprise and the different kinds of software it uses, software systems may need to be migrated once every three to six years, but no later than when the maintenance cycle for the legacy software expires.

1.1 What Is Migration?

In general, *migration* describes the replacement of a considerable portion of the software, hardware, or data that's being used. This does not refer to the act of patching software because patching doesn't alter the technical basis — usually SAP NetWeaver in the area of SAP software — in any way. During a migration process, however, the technical basis is replaced entirely. This also differentiates a migration project from an upgrade project, which merely improves the basis by promoting it to a later release status.

Example

The switchover from SAP NetWeaver 2004 to SAP NetWeaver 7.0 represents a migration. However, increasing the patch level within SAP NetWeaver, for instance, from Support Package Stack 03 (SPS) to SPS 04, is not a migration. This process is referred to as "patching" the SAP system.

A migration process consists of two different parts: the technical migration and the concept migration.

- **Technical migration**
  During a technical migration, the technical platform is replaced by a newer version. Ultimately, the technical migration "merely" consists of installing the migration package (see Chapter 2, Technical Migration).
- **Concept migration**
  The concept migration is carried out after the technical migration and includes the replacement of existing concepts and processes. New releases contain new functions that can only be used if specific requirements are met. Therefore, the

concept migration implements the new concepts and processes to meet the requirements for operating the new release and to make sure the new functions can be used (see Chapter 3, Concept Migration).

Usually, old concepts continue to be provided in a new release, but they are marked as being obsolete and are often entirely eliminated in subsequent releases. Old concepts are preserved only for reasons of compatibility and should be replaced by new ones.

Example

A technical migration involves, for example, the replacement of the SAP NetWeaver 2004 platform by SAP NetWeaver 7.0.

The concept migration in SAP NetWeaver BI implements, for example, the new data flow or replaces the old authorization concept with the new one.

There are two main reasons why you should perform a migration:

- The warranty period for your legacy system expires.
- You want to use functions of the new system that aren't available in the old system.

The following two sections describe these reasons in greater detail.

1.2 Maintenance Cycle of SAP Software

The warranty on SAP systems is subject to a firmly defined cycle, as shown in Figure 1.1.

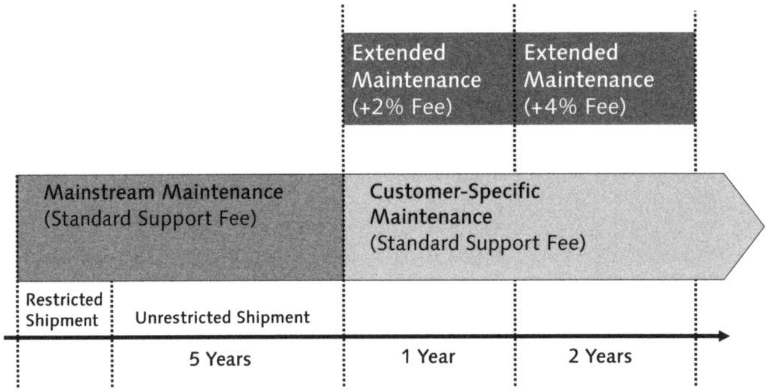

Figure 1.1 Maintenance Phases for SAP Software (Source: SAP AG)

The warranty cycle is divided into two phases: *mainstream maintenance* and *customer-specific maintenance*.

- **Mainstream maintenance**
  The mainstream maintenance period for SAP products expires after five years; customers who do not conclude any specific follow-up contract with SAP have no additional warranty claim for the software after the expiration date. This five-year period is covered by the regular SAP support contract.
- **Customer-specific maintenance**
  The additional customer-specific maintenance phase can last up to three years. The first year includes an extra charge of 2%, whereas the second and third years require an extra charge of 4% each on top of the support contract.

Consequently, the maximum duration of the warranty period for an SAP product can be eight years. After that, you must replace the system with a new version; that is, you must migrate the legacy system, provided you want to continue the maintenance cycle. The migration process upgrades the technical basis to the newest version. After this has been done, you can again wait for another eight years until the next migration becomes due.

1.3 Using New Functions

The second reason for a migration project is the requirement to use new functions that are only available in the new release. Especially in the business intelligence area, numerous new functions have been developed recently, which make a migration necessary. The following list describes some of those functions:

- **BEx Report Designer**
  The SAP Business Explorer Suite was complemented by the Report Designer. The Report Designer enables you to design reports with specific output formats, such as A4. You can also export these reports in PDF format or use them as the default print output.
- **Remodeling Toolbox**
  The Remodeling Toolbox enables you to customize InfoCubes in SAP NetWeaver BI even if the InfoCube contains data.

- **Data flow concept**
  The data flow concept of SAP BW 3.5 has been completely revised (see Section 4.1, Data Flow Concepts). Thus, InfoSources have become optional objects; update and transfer rules have been combined into transformations; and the data transfer process has been redeveloped to provide an improved error-handling functionality.
- **Real-time data acquisition**
  The new real-time data acquisition concept extracts data from source systems in real time. This technique enables you to transfer and update data with little time delay from the source system (as soon as the data is available there) to the SAP NetWeaver BI system.
- **SAP NetWeaver Portal**
  The SAP NetWeaver Portal is a new component, the use of which is mandatory for operating the BI system. SAP NetWeaver BI cannot run if you don't operate an SAP NetWeaver Portal (provided you want to use new functions). This new concept has moved many components, such as the BI Administration Cockpit and Information Broadcasting, into the portal.
- **Authorization concept**
  The authorization concept has been completely revised and designed to process more details. It now allows you to use authorizations for key figures and characteristic values (for more information on authorizations, see Chapter 5, Migrating Authorizations).
- **Drag and drop**
  The drag and drop functionality has been established in web applications. You can now modify filters and drilldowns within web applications by using drag and drop.
- **BI-integrated planning**
  The planning functionality in SAP NetWeaver BI has been completely revised. For example, the SEM-BPS component (Business Planning and Simulation) has been replaced by so-called ready-for-input queries.

You cannot use these functions of the new release until you have carried out a concept migration successfully.

The concept migration, in turn, consists of several different parts that must be processed either simultaneously or in a certain sequence. In the context of SAP NetWeaver BI, the following three tasks are relevant:

- Adapting the authorization concept
- Changing the data flow
- Redesigning the web reporting function

As you will see in Chapter 3, Concept Migration, you don't need to stick to this order when carrying out the concept migration.

1.4 How Long Does the Migration Process Take?

A migration process should be planned carefully and on time because it cannot be completed within a couple of days. For one thing, in addition to the pure software migration, you may also need to carry out a hardware migration if the minimum hardware requirements of the new release are higher or if the legacy system did not live up to your expectations. Also, a lot of things have changed in-between the different SAP software releases, which caused other interdependencies to occur between SAP components and which require comprehensive testing after the migration process has completed. This is the case in SAP NetWeaver 7.0, for example, because the SAP NetWeaver Portal has become an integral part of the software.

Depending on the products you use, the technical migration may take one to three months, whereas the concept migration can take three to 12 months, if you have to load many modules from SAP ERP 6.0 into the SAP NetWeaver BI system, for example.

With regard to the migration from SAP BW 3.5 to SAP NetWeaver BI, which is the focus of this book, the technical migration takes approximately one or two months, whereas the concept migration can take one to six months, depending on the size of the data warehouse and the number of functions used. Additional time and work may be needed if you want to implement new functions.

One of the essential benefits of migrating to SAP NetWeaver BI is that you do not have to carry out the migration process as one "big bang." This means that you don't need to implement all parts of the concept migration in a single step. Instead, you can implement individual areas separately. For example, you can change the data flow first, then put it into live operation, and continue with adjusting the authorizations afterwards.

Note that a migration from SAP BW 3.5 to SAP NetWeaver BI may also consist of the technical migration only; that is, you could replace the SAP NetWeaver platform and continue to use the old concepts. However, this is not really advisable for the following two reasons:

- You cannot use any new functions. New functions will not be released until you have migrated at least one subarea.
- You merely postpone the concept migration into the future because subsequent releases will most likely no longer support old concepts.

Tip

You should perform the concept migration in any case, but don't migrate all components at the same time, and take your time when carrying out the migration process. Chapter 3, Concept Migration, explains in detail the sequence you should follow.

1.5 Version Names

SAP BW is still often used to refer to the SAP data warehouse solution. Strictly speaking, however, SAP BW only refers to one version (see Figure 1.2).

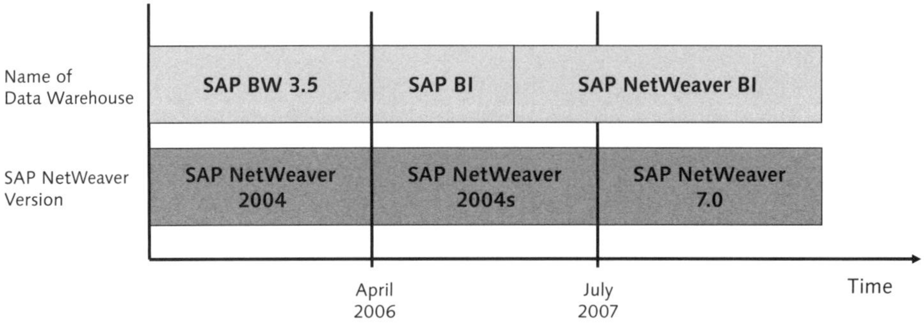

Figure 1.2 Version Names of SAP NetWeaver and the SAP Data Warehouse Solution

Earlier generations of the SAP Data Warehouse up to and including Version 3.5 were called SAP Business Information Warehouse (SAP BW). With the introduction of the new SAP NetWeaver 7.0, which was initially released as SAP NetWeaver 2004s, the name was first changed to SAP Business Intelligence (SAP BI). Around July 2007, SAP changed it again to SAP NetWeaver BI (BW 7.0).

SAP NetWeaver BI is the short form for SAP NetWeaver 7.0 Business Intelligence.

Note

In the following chapters, SAP BW is used for releases up to and including SAP BW 3.5, whereas SAP NetWeaver BI refers to the new release from SAP NetWeaver 7.0.

2 Technical Migration

This chapter focuses on the technical migration of your system landscape. For better readability and to keep the text concise, the term "migration" is used to refer to technical migration in this chapter, unless otherwise noted.

The word "migration" always involves the migration of the entire system landscape. For this reason, the chapter is divided into the following two main sections:

- **Migrating the System Landscape**
  The migration of your system landscape is based on a classical pattern, which is described in the first section.
- **Migrating Individual Systems**
  Having discussed the basic principles of migrating the system landscape, this section describes how you can migrate individual systems.

2.1 Migrating the System Landscape

As mentioned previously, the migration of a system landscape follows a classical pattern as described in this section. In fact, this general pattern can be used for SAP BW system landscapes as well as any other SAP system landscape.

A technical migration project is a very complex task that — once completed — cannot be easily undone. As a rule, the migration will take you approximately one week per SAP BW system in your system landscape. By adding the time needed for designing and testing, you should take into account a total duration of up to two months. Non-BW systems, such as SAP ERP systems, typically require even more time (up to six months).

2.1.1 Sandbox System

It makes sense to use an example to "practice" the migration project. This is particularly useful for the concept migration that will follow. This *sandbox system* represents the first system to be migrated; it is not part of your system landscape. The system should be set up on a separate server to test the migration process. Usually, the sandbox system is a copy of your live system; however, some customers use the quality assurance system as a basis (see Figure 2.1).

Names of Systems Within the System Landscape

Due to the many different names that are used within your system landscape, we'll use the following naming convention for the systems in a three-system landscape:

- **Development system**
  The first system is the one on which you carry out development tasks.
- **Quality assurance system (QA system) or test sytem**
  The second system is used for testing purposes.
- **Production system or live system**
  The third system is used for production purposes.

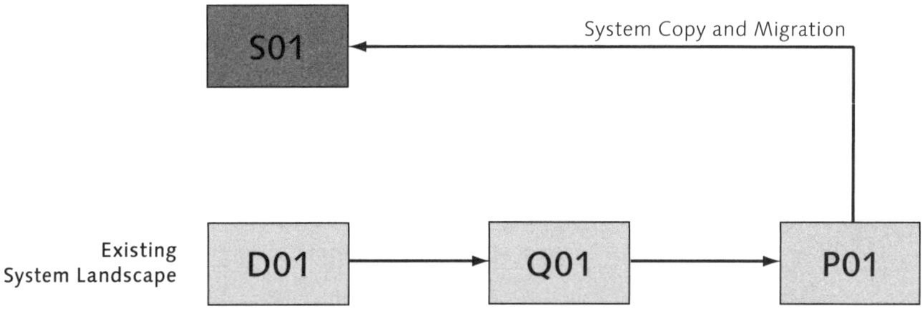

Figure 2.1 Creating a Sandbox System as a Copy of the Production System

In Figure 2.1, D01 represents the development system, Q01 the QA system, and P01 the production system. S01 stands for the new sandbox system.

Sandbox system S01 is identical to production system P01, which is the first system to be migrated after the copy process. This migration process will be described in greater detail in Section 2.2, Migrating Individual Systems. After the technical migration has completed successfully, the system will be released for consultants and developers in your enterprise to start "practicing" the concept migration.

2.1.2 Emergency Transport Track

To avoid a complete standstill of the development work in your system landscape, it is useful to create an *emergency transport track*, that is, to set up two additional systems that you can use for development purposes while the actual system landscape is being migrated. Figure 2.2 illustrates this variant.

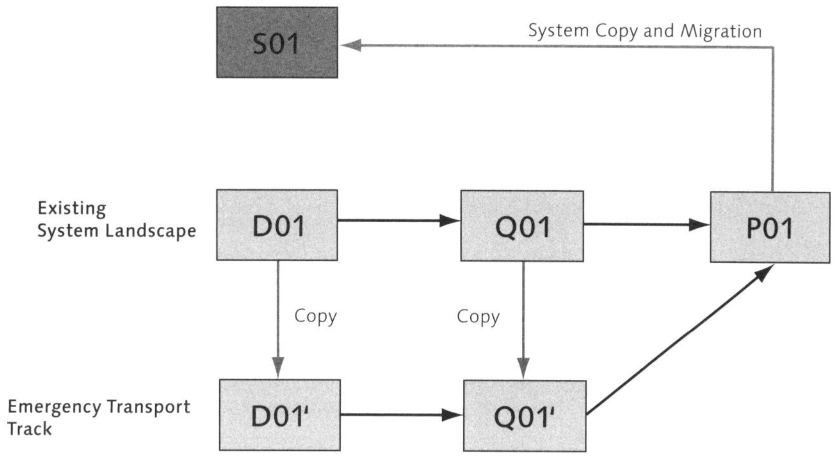

Figure 2.2 Migration via an Emergency Transport Track

Systems D01' and Q01' are exact copies of the original systems, D01 and Q01, and are excluded from the migration process. These systems are used for development purposes and will be removed after the migration process is finished. As soon as the system copies have been created, you can start migrating the existing system landscape (see Figure 2.3).

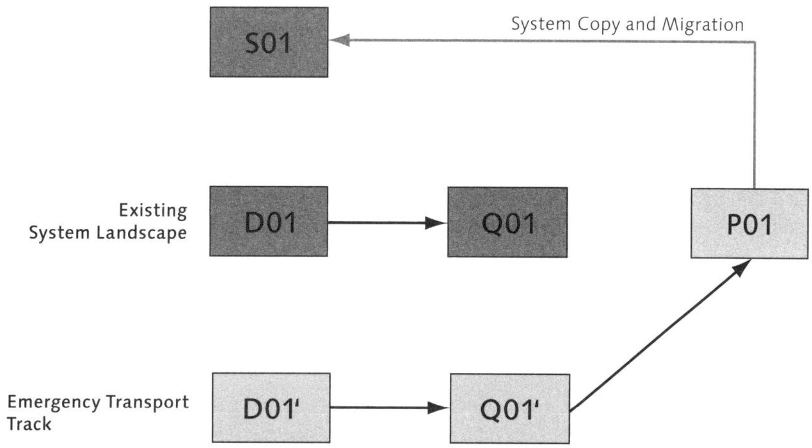

Figure 2.3 Migrating the System Landscape

As shown in Figure 2.3, the transport route from Q01 to P01 is temporarily disconnected because transports from systems with a higher SAP Basis release to systems with a lower SAP Basis release should not be carried out. This is usually not possible anyway. The differences between the two systems are too big for a transport to work. At this point, the emergency transport track comes into play, which you can use to continue developing as before.

At this stage, the D01 and Q01 systems have already been migrated, whereas production system P01 and the systems of the emergency transport track, D01' and Q01', are still located on the old release. The production system won't be migrated until the D01 and Q01 systems, as well as the transport route in-between the two, have been tested successfully (see Figure 2.4).

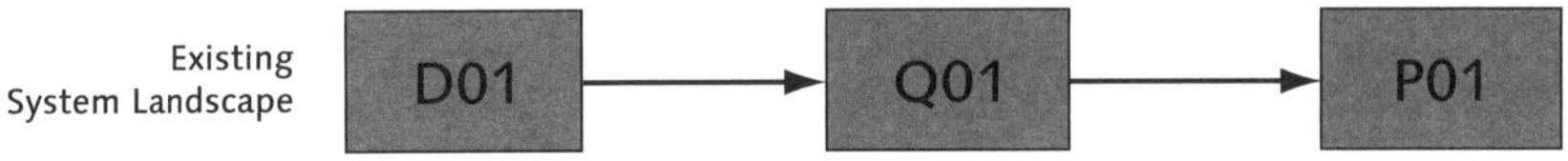

Figure 2.4 System Landscape After Successful Migration

To do that, you must first remove the transport route of the emergency transport track and reconnect the old system landscape — now on the new release (e.g., SAP NetWeaver BI) — with the production system. After that, the D01' and Q01' systems, as well as the sandbox system, S01, should be removed. Some companies continue to use the sandbox system for a while, depending on whether additional tests are supposed to be carried out.

What follows next is the comprehensive post-migration maintenance work mentioned at the beginning, which is caused by the emergency transport track. During the migration process, the entire development work was carried out on the surrogate systems, D01' and Q01', but not on the systems of your system landscape, D01 and Q01. Consequently, production system P01 has a newer status than D01 and Q01; that is, the versioning within your system landscape is incorrect. Therefore, it is mandatory to apply all changes that were made on D01' and Q01' to the D01 and Q01 systems as well, which can be a very complex endeavor, depending on the number of developments made.

2.1.3 "Frozen Zone" Variant

Sometimes, customers decide against the emergency transport track because it is time-consuming and requires new hardware. The third argument against it is the increased maintenance work during and after the migration process. For this reason, you can also use a different variant, the so-called *frozen zone*. As the name suggests, in a frozen zone, the systems of the system landscape are locked during the migration process. During the course of the migration, you must not carry out any development work or transports within your system landscape. The advantage of this is that no additional systems and servers are needed; however, no development work can take place for the duration of the migration process.

2.1.4 Conclusion and Recommendation

Your decision as to which variant you want to use should be based on the specific situation. If you cannot halt all of your development tasks, you should opt for the emergency transport track. Especially in large enterprises, it's then essential to order the required new hardware as early as possible because the ordering process usually involves many approval steps.

However, if it isn't a problem in your company to stop all development work entirely for a period of three to four weeks, then you should declare the three systems a frozen zone and forbid all developments. This is by all means the most cost-efficient and least work-intensive way.

Excursus: Migration to SAP ERP 6.0

In migrations from SAP ERP systems, such as SAP R/3 4.6C, to the new Release SAP ERP 6.0, the technical migration takes several months. In that case, you should always use the emergency transport track variant because a development standstill for such a long period of time is impossible.

2.2 Migrating Individual Systems

Let's now consider the migration of an individual system from your system landscape. You must carry out this procedure for each system in your system landscape to upgrade your system landscape to the new release SAP NetWeaver BI.

2.2.1 Basic Principles

Usually, the SAP Basis department in your company carries out the technical migration of each individual system. The process consists of several steps recommended by SAP. SAP provides an *Upgrade Master Guide* for each new release that describes the process of the technical migration. This chapter describes the principle steps, which are always up-to-date. Refer to the *Master Guide* for individual reports and tips.

Upgrade Master Guide

The *Master Guide* is available in the SAP Service Marketplace under the */instguides* quicklink. To get there, visit *https://service.sap.com/instguides*, and navigate through the menu on the left. Then choose INSTALLATION & UPGRADE GUIDES • SAP NETWEAVER • SAP NETWEAVER 7.0 (2004S) • UPGRADE. Then, a reference to the *Upgrade Master Guide* displays in the Planning section.

The *Upgrade Master Guide* contains all of the steps required for the migration. The migration of individual systems is based on the following procedure:

- Planning the migration and performing prechecks to check whether all requirements for a migration are met
- Preparing the technical migration (Preparation)
- Performing the technical migration (Upgrade)
- Post-processing the technical migration (Post Activities), which also serves to prepare the concept migration

The contents of the individual phases are clearly defined and should be strictly adhered to. Each phase of the migration contains a comprehensive list of SAP Notes from the SAP Service Marketplace that can be used for troubleshooting, correcting errors, or retrieving information. The SAP Notes are a useful complement to the *Upgrade Master Guide*.

Recommendation

You should strictly adhere to the migration processes defined by SAP by following the *Upgrade Master Guide*. If necessary, consult with external specialists to obtain expert support.

2.2.2 Planning and Preparation

The migration project begins with planning, where you work out the steps you'll have to carry out. As described in Chapter 1, Basic Principles of Migration, SAP NetWeaver 7.0 requires the operation of an SAP NetWeaver Portal (provided you want to use new functions in reporting). Apart from that, you must migrate several other objects as listed here:

- Upgrade the database of your SAP BW system.
- Upgrade the Application Server ABAP to SAP NetWeaver 7.0.
- Install/upgrade an Application Server Java with usage type "BI Java" and "EP" (Enterprise Portal).
- Activate the BEx Web environment to operate the SAP Business Explorer Suite.
- Activate (optional) the technical content and monitoring tools, such as the BI Administration Cockpit.

As mentioned, SAP provides a long list of SAP Notes on the topic of migration for each phase. The complete lists are contained in the *Upgrade Master Guide*, sorted by subject matter.

After you know which tasks you'll need to perform during the migration phase, you can start preparing the migration:

- **Transport system and users**
  Prior to starting the migration process, you should either release and transport or delete all open transport requests. After that, you should forbid the creation of transport requests for the duration of the migration process and prevent all non-SAP Basis users that are directly involved in the migration (developers, administrators, etc.) from logging in to the system.
- **Background processes**
  Furthermore, you must stop all background processes during the migration phase because they could hamper the process. You can delete or deallocate background processes using Report RSBTCDEL2 (see Figure 2.5). See also, SAP Note 784969 on this topic.

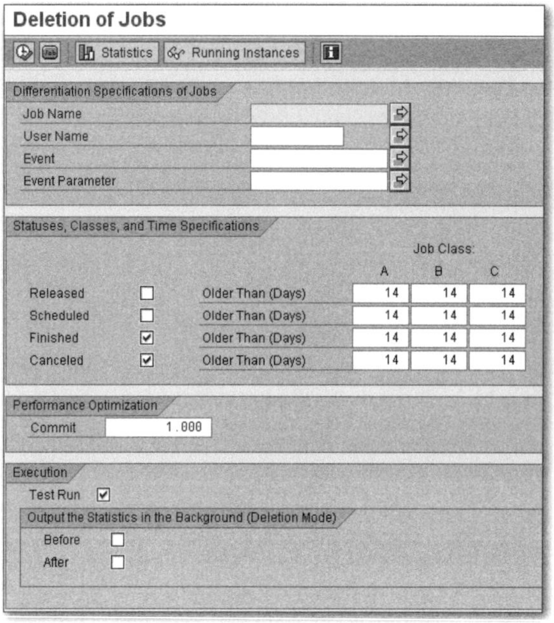

Figure 2.5 Deleting Background Jobs via Report RSBTCDEL2

- **Repairing InfoObjects**
  To avoid a loss of data during the migration process, you should activate and check all InfoObjects. To do that, start Transaction RSD1, and select all InfoObjects. Then activate all InfoObjects that are not highlighted in green. Moreover, all other objects such as InfoCubes and so on should be active as well. For this purpose, you can use the RSUPGRCHECK report (see Figure 2.6), which checks your BW system for active and inactive versions. See also SAP Note 1032367 on this topic.

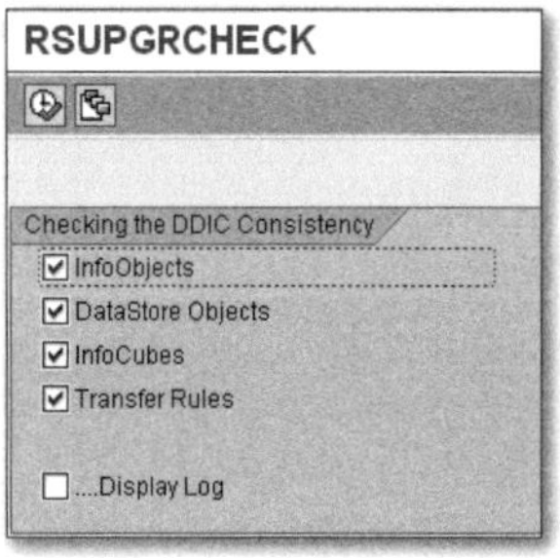

Figure 2.6 Comprehensive Upgrade Check of the SAP BW System

- **Consistency of master data**
  Prior to upgrading to SAP NetWeaver BI, you should check your master data for consistency by using Report RSDMD_CHECKPRG_ALL (see Figure 2.7). However, note that you should always select subsets of your InfoObjects to avoid long runtimes and potential aborts.

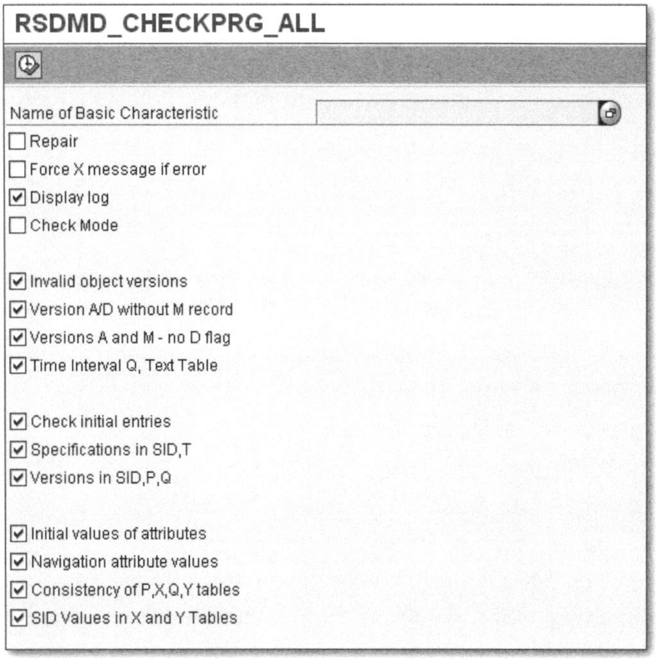

Figure 2.7 Report RSDMD_CHECKPRG_ALL for Checking Master Data Consistency

- **Additional consistency checks**
  The ANALYZE_RSZ_TABLE report enables you to carry out additional consistency checks for your SAP BW system. This report checks internal SAP BW tables for consistency. See also SAP Notes 792779, 966080, and 1020826 on this topic.
- **Activating and repairing ODS objects**
  After upgrading from SAP BW 3.5 to SAP NetWeaver BI, you'll notice that ODS objects do not exist anymore. To avoid this problem, you should make sure that all ODS objects are active before starting the migration. After that, run Report RSDG_ODSO_ACTIVATE (see Figure 2.8), and read SAP Note 861890.

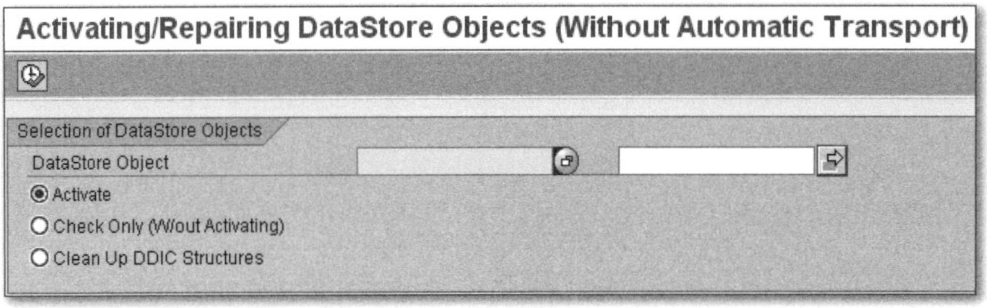

Figure 2.8 Repairing and Activating ODS Objects (Report RSDG_ODSO_ACTIVATE)

After you have completed all preparatory work, you can start the migration process. For this purpose, you should download the necessary software from the SAP Service Marketplace.

- **Database and transport system**
  Download database release needed for SAP NetWeaver BI. You can find it in the SAP Service Marketplace under */patches*. You should also download the latest transport files, which are located in the same directory.
- **SAP GUI**
  To use all functions after the upgrade, you need a new SAP GUI. You need at least SAP GUI 6.40 Compilation 5 as well as .NET Framework 1.1 to continue your daily work. The .NET Framework is required to activate the SAP NetWeaver BI component in SAP GUI, which contains the new SAP Business Explorer Suite (for more information on SAP GUI and the required versions, see Section 2.2.5, Using SAP GUI).
- **Support packages**
  Download the currently available support packages for SAP NetWeaver 7.0, which are also located under the */patches* quicklink in the SAP Service Marketplace. Experience has shown that you should never choose the latest support package. Therefore, always stay one or two release statuses below the currently available support package.
- **SPAM/SAINT updates**
  As a rule, you should always install the latest SPAM/SAINT updates in your SAP BW system before starting the migration process.

Important Note

After upgrading the system to SAP NetWeaver 7.0 BI, you usually need to patch it; that is, you must install new support packages. Choose your target support package with care, and stick to the following rules:

- Do not choose the latest support package available.
- SAP strictly recommends discontinuing the use of Support Packages 11 through 13. Therefore, you should install Support Package 10 or 14.

As mentioned earlier, it's necessary to run an SAP NetWeaver Portal. If you already have an older version of the SAP Java Engine, you can upgrade and use it (Java Engine Version 6.30 or higher); otherwise, you must install the new Java Engine 7.00. In any case, you should refer to SAP Notes 927255 and 853572.

SAP NetWeaver 7.0 also causes a change in the directory structure on your server. In this context, you should refer to SAP Note 919046, which describes how to migrate to the new structure.

When you have completed all preparatory tasks, you can start upgrading your system.

2.2.3 Preparing and Upgrading the System

The upgrade process for your SAP BW system starts by executing the PREPARE command at the operating system level. This command is part of the upgrade tools available from the SAP Service Marketplace. Note that when you execute this command, the system creates log files of up to 10GB. For more information on this topic, see SAP Notes 762426, 96317, and 816211.

The upgrade wizard has turned into a graphical tool that facilitates the upgrade process considerably. In the first step, you must select the administrator user on the system, who is supposed to carry out the upgrade. After that, you must specify which PI_BASIS package you want to use. SAP Notes 539977 and 557584 contain valuable tips and information about the requirements in this context.

During the course of the upgrade process, the upgrade wizard prompts you for various passwords. The passwords, also referred to as upgrade keywords, are contained in the *Upgrade Master Guide*:

- Upgrade keyword for SAP Basis 7.00: 20746614
- Upgrade keyword for SAP Basis 7.00 SR1: 24623123

- Upgrade keyword for SAP Basis 7.00 SR2: 30546999
- Upgrade keyword for SAP Business Content 7.02: 4075693
- Upgrade keyword for SAP Business Content 7.03: 3740746
- Upgrade keyword for SEM/Finbasis: 4735387
- Upgrade keyword for the ST-A/PI component: Contained in SAP Note 597673

During the upgrade process, the wizard asks you whether you want to use new security policies and tools. Here, you should follow the instructions displayed onscreen and read the respective messages to get an overview of the entire functionality.

As is the case with initial installations of SAP systems, you can never be sure that the system won't crash. However, numerous SAP Notes are available that provide detailed information on error messages that may occur during the upgrade process. You can find a list of these SAP Notes in the respective places in the *Upgrade Master Guide*.

2.2.4 Post-Processing the Migration

After the successful system migration, you must carry out some follow-up tasks to complete the process entirely. Refer to the *Upgrade Master Guide* for more detailed information about this topic.

- **SAP Load Generator**
  You can access the SAP Load Generator via Transaction SGEN to precompile programs and transactions (see Figure 2.9). If you forget to call this transaction, the initial call of Transaction RSA1 may well take 20 to 30 minutes.
- **Conversion errors during the upgrade**
  Check for conversion errors in the *longpost.log* file that was created during the upgrade process. If you find conversion errors, you should proceed as described in SAP Note 197886.
- **Starting background processes**
  You must restart the background processes that were stopped at the beginning of the upgrade process. To do that, run report BTCTRNS2 with user DDIC in client 000.

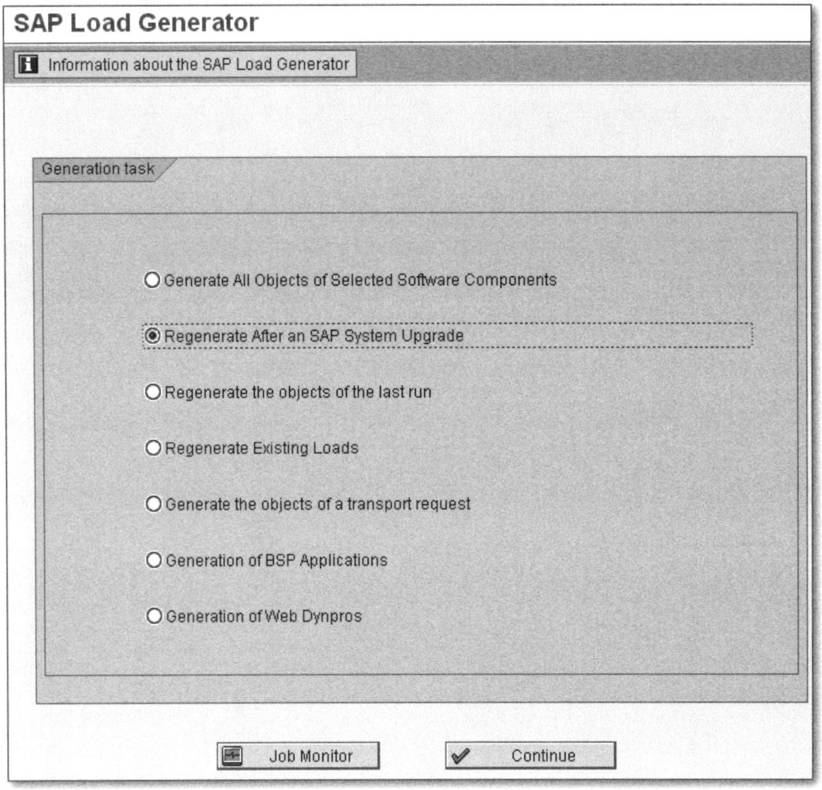

Figure 2.9 SAP Load Generator, Transaction SGEN

- **New SAP Crypto Library**
  Download the latest version of the SAP Crypto Library, which is located in the SAP Service Marketplace under the */tcs* quicklink.
- **SPAM/SAINT updates**
  After the migration process is finished, you should install the latest SPAM/SAINT updates in your SAP NetWeaver BI system prior to installing new support packages.

Furthermore, SAP recommends migrating the authorizations to the new concept (see Chapter 5, Migrating Authorizations). If you don't want to do that, you must activate the old authorization concept after the system upgrade. By default, the system is set to the new authorization concept after the migration process (see Figure 2.10).

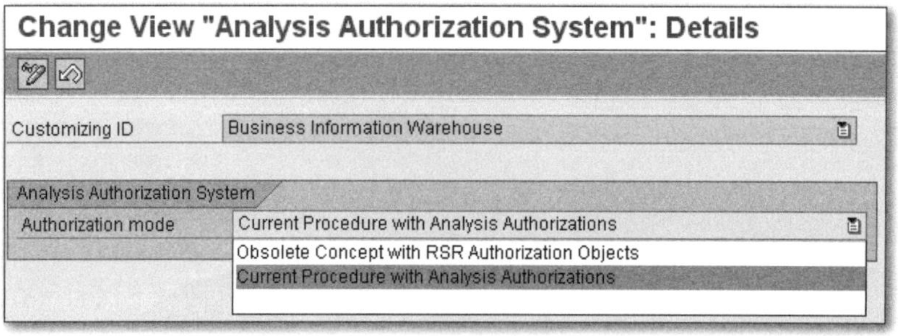

Figure 2.10 Selecting the Authorization System

You can set the authorization concept in the Implementation Guide (IMG) (Transaction SPRO) under SAP NETWEAVER • BUSINESS INTELLIGENCE • SETTINGS FOR REPORTING AND ANALYSIS • GENERAL SETTINGS FOR REPORTING AND ANALYSIS • ANALYSIS AUTHORIZATIONS: SELECT CONCEPT.

All additional tasks to be carried out are specified in the Upgrade Master Guide. On one hand, these tasks are related to the database, on the other hand, they "merely" consist of executing (approx. 25 to 30) reports. The Upgrade Master Guide always contains an up-to-date list of these reports.

2.2.5 Using SAP GUI

After the migration, you must use SAP GUI 6.40 Compilation 5 or higher for the system to operate accurately. Otherwise, you can't use the new Business Explorer Suite and basic functions in the Data Warehousing Workbench. Therefore, many customers use the new version, SAP GUI 7.10, if they need to replace SAP GUI anyway.

Although this is a viable choice, you should take into account the minimum requirements for SAP GUI 7.10, provided you use Windows XP as your client operating system:

- You must use Microsoft Office XP (2002) SP2 or higher.
- To support Microsoft Office XP SP2, SAP GUI 7.10 Frontend Patch 3 or higher must be installed.
- SAP GUI 7.10 requires .NET Framework 2.0 (in contrast to SAP GUI 6.40, which requires only .NET Framework 1.1).

In one of our customer projects, the distribution of SAP GUI 7.10 caused a lot of problems due to the first of the preceding requirements because we hadn't planned to install SP2 for Office XP.

On Windows Vista machines, you must always use SAP GUI 7.10 because this operating system no longer supports SAP GUI 6.40.

2.3 Summary

This chapter described how to carry out a technical migration. It started with a general description of how you should migrate a system landscape. Every migration process starts with a sandbox system, that is, a system that is set up for the purpose of practicing. After that, you can carry out the migration either via an emergency transport track or by creating frozen zones. Depending on the size of the system and the necessity of development work that runs in parallel to the migration process, you should determine which of the two variants meets your requirements better.

The chapter then described how to migrate an individual system. In this context, you learned about the Upgrade Master Guide as a central document that always contains the most up-to-date information.

The migration process itself consists of the following four phases:

- Planning the migration, including a check of the migration requirements
- Preparing the technical migration (Preparation)
- Performing the technical migration (Upgrade)
- Post-processing the technical migration (Post Activities)

The planning phase is the most important one because you check whether a migration is feasible. This phase is followed by the preparation and execution of the migration, both of which take place at the operating system level. After a successful migration, you must carry out several post-processing tasks to remove errors that may have occurred and to make the system usable.

3 Concept (Functional) Migration

After you have technically upgraded the SAP BW system to SAP NetWeaver BI, you can start migrating the feature.

This chapter introduces and describes concept, or function migration as well as the work steps it involves. After that, you'll learn about the individual areas to be migrated and get a detailed overview of the migration process.

Naming Convention

In the following section, concept migration is referred to simply as the "migration," unless otherwise noted.

3.1 Introduction to Concept Migration

Usually, the concept migration immediately follows the technical migration. Whereas the technical migration upgrades the system technically to the new release SAP NetWeaver BI, the concept migration implements the new concepts, or function that come with SAP NetWeaver BI:

- Data flow concept
- Authorization concept
- Reporting

Note that carrying out the concept migration is not mandatory. All features and procedures that you know from SAP BW are still supported; however, SAP does not develop them any further. Furthermore, you cannot use the new functions provided in SAP NetWeaver BI until you have implemented the new features. Consequently, if you want to use new functions contained in one of the three new features, you must perform the concept migration for the relevant area.

> **Reasons for Migration**
>
> You only need to carry out a concept migration if you want to use new functions in SAP NetWeaver BI. You only need to migrate the respective area — data flow, authorizations, or reporting — from which you want to use new functions.

The following sections provide a brief description of the three areas, including the differences from the previous release.

3.1.1 Data Flow

The data flow comprises the entire ETL process (Extraction Transformation Loading), which extracts data from a source system, then transforms and cleanses the data, and finally updates the data into InfoProviders.

The data flow consists of the following objects you should already know from SAP BW: DataSource, transfer rule, InfoSource, update rule, and InfoProviders, such as InfoCubes or ODS objects.

The following areas have been completely redesigned:

- The InfoSource is no longer a mandatory object but optional.
- The transfer and update rules have been combined into what is referred to as the transformation.
- The InfoPackage is used only for requesting data from the source system. The new data transfer process (DTP) is used to update data to the data targets. The DTP contains improved and new error-handling methods.
- The underlying ABAP programming language was replaced by its object-oriented variant, ABAP Objects.

In addition to these substantial changes, some other minor changes should be mentioned:

- The modeling of InfoCubes was made similar to that of ODS objects.
- The ODS object was renamed to SAP NetWeaver BI DataStore object (DSO). The functionality of the object hasn't changed at all and was complemented by a write-optimized DSO.
- Transformations can now be modeled graphically by linking source and target fields with each other via drag and drop. Moreover, transformations not

only contain a start routine but also the new end routine, and you now have the option to control transformations entirely through ABAP routines (expert routines).

- The flow of data from a DataSource to an InfoProvider is now directly displayed in a tree structure within the RSA1. However, the Display Data Flow option continues to be available.
- The Reporting Agent has been eliminated and can only be accessed via Information Broadcasting in the SAP NetWeaver Portal.
- The persistent staging area (PSA) is now linked with the DataSource and no longer with the transfer rule or the new transformation.

The migration process itself is more or less automatic and is integrated in Transaction RSA1. This transaction enables you to either create new objects for each old object or migrate your old objects. However, due to the switchover from ABAP to ABAP Objects this process involves some manual post-processing work that shouldn't be underestimated.

For more information on the new and old data flow concepts as well as on the migration process, refer to Chapter 4, Migrating the Data Flow.

3.1.2 Authorizations

Authorizations are intended to protect sensitive data against unauthorized access. The reporting authorizations that you already know from SAP BW fulfill this purpose, and you can use them for managing your authorizations. These reporting authorizations are based on the known SAP authorization objects.

In SAP NetWeaver BI, the reporting authorization was replaced with analysis authorization. The main difference between these two types of authorization is that the analysis authorization is no longer based on authorization objects, but it represents a separate new model for maintaining authorizations. In general, authorizations continue to be controlled at a very detailed level. The following five levels are available for authorization control:

- At InfoCube level
- At characteristic level
- At characteristic value level

- At key figure level
- At hierarchy node level

The process of maintaining authorizations at hierarchy node level is now identical to maintaining value authorizations from an analysis authorization; both processes can be controlled via the same transaction. The use of InfoObject 0TCTAUTHH for maintenance purposes has been completely done away with.

The migration process is controlled via ABAP Report RSEC_MIGRATION, which runs automatically. Depending on the level of complexity of your current authorization concept, the automatic migration process may require some manual post-processing.

For further information on migrating the authorization concept and a description of both concepts, see Chapter 5, Migrating Authorizations.

3.1.3 Reporting

Migrating the reporting system is by far the most complex task within the concept migration procedure because SAP has moved reporting entirely to the SAP NetWeaver Portal. Compared to previous releases, this provides you with many additional options to implement your specific reporting requirements; however, note that SAP also removed some of the functions due to the shift into the SAP NetWeaver Portal.

The most fundamental changes related to the SAP NetWeaver BI reporting system include the following:

- The move of the reporting system into the SAP NetWeaver Portal.
- The new BEx Report Designer as a reporting tool that enables you to design custom reports with specific output formats, such as A4.
- A complete redevelopment of the Business Explorer Suite, which consists of the BEx Analyzer, BEx Query Designer, BEx Web Application Designer, and the BEx Report Designer.
- The relocation of Information Broadcasting, role menu, and ABC analysis into the SAP NetWeaver Portal. The preliminary calculation via the Reporting Agent is now also controlled through Information Broadcasting.

See Chapter 6, Migration in Reporting, for more detailed information on the reporting functions as well as the migration process.

The following section provides a detailed description of the three areas — data flow, authorizations, and reporting — and discusses the migration principle in general.

3.2 Basic Principles and Flow of the Concept Migration

In contrast to the technical migration, the concept migration does not have to follow a strict sequence with regard to migrating specific areas. It's up to you to decide when you want to migrate which of the three areas — data flow, authorizations, and reporting — or whether you want to do that *at all*.

You should migrate only the parts that you actually *want* to migrate. For example, if the new web reporting function is important for you, you should migrate it right at the start or even migrate only this part and nothing else. Or if you want to carry out only the technical migration to upgrade to the latest release status, you can do that without any problem. However, you should bear in mind that although SAP continues to support all old concepts, it doesn't develop them any further. Thus, it is possible that old concepts will be eliminated entirely in releases that follow SAP NetWeaver 7.0.

Therefore, you should decide on which areas you want to migrate prior to starting the whole migration project. Depending on the capacities available to you, you should then carry out the individual migration steps either simultaneously or one after the other.

3.2.1 Migration Sequence

Experience has shown that it makes sense to perform the concept migration in a single process; however, due to the freedom you have regarding which areas of a system landscape you want to migrate, companies usually take their time for the implementation. The essential advantage of this approach is that it allows you to verify, implement, and test every single concept. The implementation as a "big bang" is not necessary and by no means advisable.

In its slide collections for the technical migration (see Appendix A, Bibliography), SAP recommends migrating the authorization concept immediately after the technical migration. This makes a lot of sense. The authorization system is by far the most sensitive element in an SAP NetWeaver BI system, and it must therefore be tested extensively. Consequently, you should start the migration project in your company by migrating the authorizations first, in collaboration with the SAP Basis department.

After you have done that, it's difficult to tell which steps should follow next. In any case, you should migrate those parts first that are most important to you. For example, if you want to make use of new reports and concepts, you should start by implementing the web reporting function. However, if you want to benefit from the advantages of the error-handling function in data updates, you should first migrate the data flow and thus implement data transfer processes.

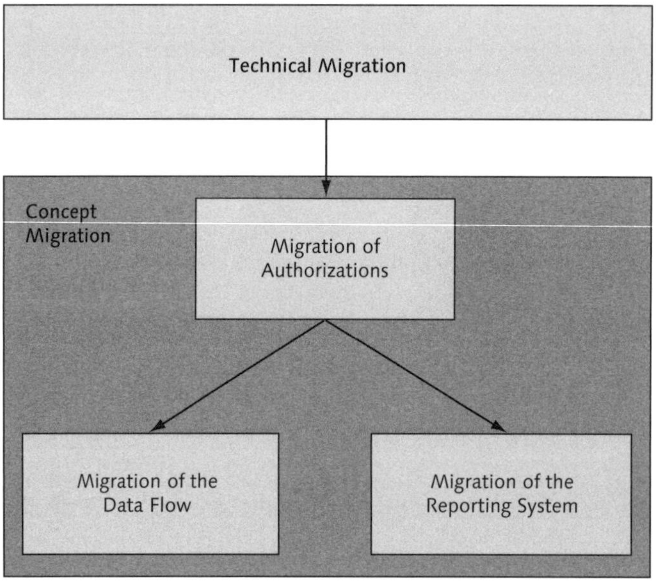

Figure 3.1 Recommended Sequence of Steps in Concept Migration

If your system capacities are sufficient, you should opt for a simultaneous migration of both the data flow and the reporting system (see Figure 3.1).

3.2.2 Migration Principle

Each part of the migration process should adhere to the following principle: none of the old objects must be overwritten or replaced; instead, all objects must first be copied and then migrated.

Preserving the Old Concepts

All original objects are left unchanged during the migration process. Instead, the objects are copied and then created with new technical names.

Each area is migrated in a different manner:

- **Authorization concept**
  The migration of the authorization concept starts automatically with the execution of an ABAP report (RSEC_MIGRATION). In some cases, it may be necessary to carry out some post-processing work.
- **Data flow concept**
  The new data flow concept is carried out separately for each data flow. The migration itself runs more or less automatically; however, note that activating the newly created objects requires some manual work if you have used custom routines for their implementation.
- **Reporting**
  The migration of the reporting system consists of two different parts: the completely automatic and optional migration of a query, followed by the migration of a web application. The migration of the web application is initiated using a migration tool; however, unfortunately this tool usually reaches its limits very quickly if reports become too complex. For more information on this, see Chapter 6, Migration in Reporting.

Authorizations are migrated using a multistep ABAP report, which you must first provide with users whose authorizations you want to migrate. Here, you must specify all users who belong to a user group. After you've done that, the migration process runs automatically based on the method you selected.

Depending on the level of complexity of your authorization concept, some manual post-processing may be necessary. Simple concepts, on the other hand, can be implemented using the ABAP report; however, you should always test these concepts extensively afterward.

For further information on migrating authorizations, refer to Chapter 5, Migrating Authorizations.

Data flows must always be migrated individually. Thus you can carry out the migration step by step and customize and test each transformation separately. Post-processing work becomes necessary whenever you use ABAP in start routines or rules because in SAP NetWeaver BI, the basic programming language is ABAP Objects and no longer ABAP. Depending on the level of complexity of the routines you use, the migration effort may increase considerably. For detailed information on the exact procedures and the amount of work involved, refer to Chapter 4, Migrating the Data Flow.

In reporting, the migration process consists of the automatic migration of queries. Because SAP NetWeaver BI can process queries created in SAP BW 3.5, this step is optional. However, if you do want to migrate a query, then note the exception to the preceding rule in the following box.

Migrating Queries

After you have migrated a query, you can no longer open it using old tools. Thus, the query is the only object that is overwritten during the migration process, provided you save it under the same name.

After the optional query migration, you can migrate web applications, if you have any. To start this process, you must use a migration tool that's integrated in the BEx Web Application Designer. However, note that this process requires some considerable manual post-processing work, which shouldn't be underestimated. This work, in turn, consists of the concept migration itself, which reestablishes the functionality of the system after the migration process, and of the optical migration, which adapts the layout to the SAP NetWeaver Portal after the migration. For further information on migrating the reporting system, see Chapter 6, Migration in Reporting.

3.3 Summary

This chapter described the concept migration. You learned that you can migrate the following three different concepts:

- Data flow concept
- Authorization concept
- Reporting

These three concepts can be migrated independently, but SAP recommends migrating the authorization concept immediately after the technical migration.

Having described the three concepts and their new features, the chapter then covered the sequence and overall flow of the migration process. To a wide extent, the authorization concept is migrated automatically by means of an ABAP report. Data flows are migrated individually and automatically but must be customized due to the changeover from ABAP to ABAP Objects. The reporting system begins with the optional and automatic migration of a query. After that, you can migrate web applications into the new version by using a migration tool. Note that this requires a considerable amount of manual work.

4 Migrating the Data Flow

This chapter explains how to migrate the data flow by first introducing you to the concepts of data flow from SAP BW and SAP NetWeaver BI and then familiarizing you with the migration method. Finally, you will see a simple and a complex migration project as well as a cost estimate and real-life observations.

4.1 Data Flow Concepts

To migrate the data flow, it's essential that you understand the data flow concepts of both the old and new releases before you start and are able to differentiate between them because these differences cause difficulties at certain points of the migration.

The chapter begins by explaining both the SAP BW 3.x and the SAP NetWeaver BI data flow concepts in more detail. This will also provide newcomers to this topic with a good overview. Section 4.1.3 follows this, highlighting the differences between the two concepts.

Naming Convention

In the following sections, the term "3.x data flow concept" refers to the data flow concept up to and including SAP BW 3.5. The term "7.0 data flow concept" refers to the new data flow concept from SAP NetWeaver BI.

An SAP BW system is used to extract information from several source systems, cleanse it (to transform it), enrich it, and hence make it available for reporting that is not dependent on any particular source system. In an SAP BW system, different object types are available for high-performance analysis and consolidated data storage; the two most important ones are the Operational DataStore object (ODS object) and the InfoCube.

Note

The ODS object has been referred to as a DataStore object (DSO) since the SAP NetWeaver BI release. Because we're currently discussing the 3.x data flow, the terms that apply to this release will also be used.

The greatest difference between the ODS object and the InfoCube lies in the type of data storage. ODS objects are generally made up of three relational database tables (active data, new data, and change log); the InfoCube, on the other hand, is based on the SAP enhanced star schema, which is used for storing multidimensional structures in relational databases. Depending on the size of the InfoCube, database tables can emerge here in high double figures.

The multidimensional database model is another type of data storage. It's optimized for reporting and allows more flexible analysis options than "normal" database tables. Therefore, you can combine each field within an InfoCube with any other field, and underlying key figures are still given the correct values.

This is why it's essential to transform the data from the mostly relationally structured source systems to the multidimensional structures, which is a very time-consuming process.

Besides transforming the data to the multidimensional database model, data in the source systems usually exists in different formats.

Example

Source system 1 saves a date in the format YYYYMMDD in the database; source system 2, on the other hand, uses the internal display DDMMYYYY. You need to decide on one format to be used in reporting. The other format is transformed accordingly.

Consequently, the data provided by the source system must as a rule be cleansed and consolidated to ensure a standard format in reporting.

SAP BW 3.5 and SAP NetWeaver BI do this in exactly the same way; the 3.x data flow concept has, however, been further developed and honed over the years. Objects became obsolete, new objects were added, and objects have become optional. In the following sections, you'll see what the concepts look like and what has changed.

Definition of Terms

If you are unsure about some of the terms used in the following sections, the majority of them are explained in the glossary.

4.1.1 3.x Data Flow Concept

Figure 4.1 outlines the basic framework of the 3.x data flow concept.

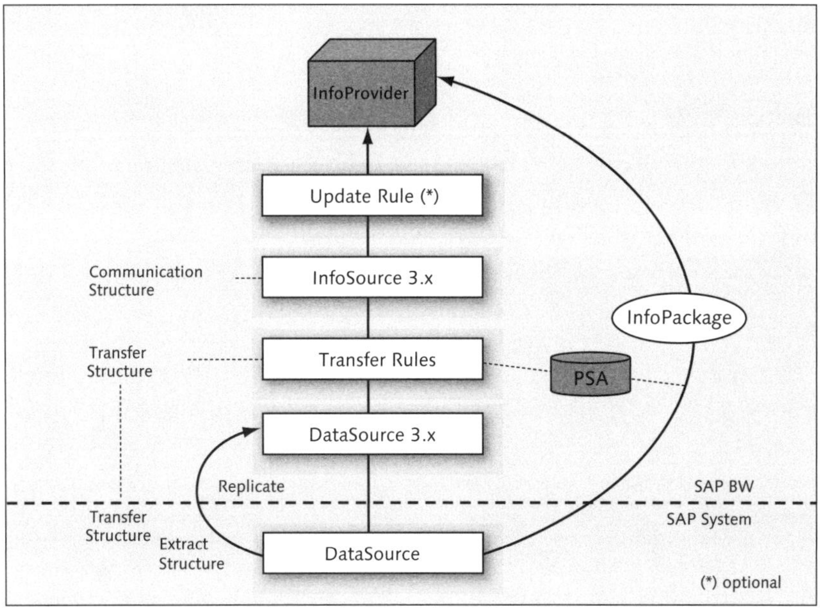

Figure 4.1 Overview of the 3.x Data Flow

The figure is divided into two areas. The lower part shows an SAP system as a source system; the upper part contains the SAP BW system.

DataSource

The data flow always begins with a *DataSource*. A DataSource is a set of fields that are provided for transferring data to the SAP BW system. Using the Service API (SAPI), which contains the programs for extracting data from SAP source systems, there is a special feature that allows the DataSource to be created directly in the source system. In all other source systems, the DataSource is created in the SAP BW system.

Extraction Structure

The DataSource has an *extraction structure*, which contains the field catalog of the fields to be extracted. The extraction can be implemented using database tables, views, or function modules. For database tables or views, it makes sense to use objects that are already available; you can hide fields that are not required in the DataSource maintenance.

Transfer Structure

You can reduce the number of fields to be extracted before they are transferred to the SAP BW system if, for example, not all of the fields are required in SAP BW. The subset of these fields is called the *transfer structure*.

Replication

For an SAP source system, the DataSource and the related transfer structure must be introduced to SAP BW after they have been created. This is called the *replication* process, which passes the transfer structure on to the SAP BW system so it is available for use.

References to the Objects

To make it easier to understand and differentiate the new SAP NetWeaver BI release from the old one, objects that were available in both releases are referred to in this chapter as "object 3.x" for SAP BW 3.x and "object" for SAP NetWeaver BI. The objects are referred to in exactly the same way in SAP NetWeaver BI.

InfoSource 3.x

The data in the 3.x data flow concept can only be transferred if an InfoSource 3.x is assigned to the DataSource 3.x, whose fields are assigned to one another within the transfer rules. The use of the InfoSource 3.x and the transfer rules is mandatory.

Like a DataSource 3.x, the *InfoSource 3.x* has a large number of fields that are available as InfoObjects. It is, however, just a structure description and does not physically contain any data. It is used for transforming and consolidating the data delivered from the DataSource and can be supplied with data from multiple DataSources. It is linked to the transfer rules and is activated when these rules are activated. The same applies to the DataSource 3.x, which is also linked to the transfer rules. The field catalog of the InfoSource 3.x, which is based on InfoObjects, is referred to as the *communication structure*.

Transfer Rules/PSA

The *transfer rule* is a central object in the 3.x data flow concept. When you activate the transfer rule, besides activating the DataSource 3.x and the InfoSource 3.x, you also activate the *persistent staging area* (PSA). This activates all runtime objects. The PSA is a relational database table that physically receives the data from the source system. It is made up of the fields from the transfer structure of the DataSource 3.x.

In Figure 4.1, the *PSA* object is highlighted in dark gray; it's the first object to physically carry data. It's also referred to as the persistent object, like the InfoProvider in this figure too.

Transfer Options

Within the transfer rules, fields can be allocated using assignments, formulas, or ABAP routines. There are hardly any limits to transformation.

Update Rules

After you've created the InfoSource 3.x and activated the transfer rules, the data can be updated in InfoProviders, such as InfoCubes or ODS objects, after it has been transformed and cleansed. You do this using the *update rules* that have the same name, which are linked with an InfoSource 3.x.

Like transfer rules, update rules are transformations that update the data as a communication structure of the InfoSource 3.x in InfoCubes or ODS objects using assignments, formulas, or ABAP routines. They always write in persistent objects.

InfoPackage

Alongside the 3.x data flow runs the *InfoPackage*, which is used both for requesting data in the source system and for updating it in the data targets. It accompanies the entire data flow from the DataSource 3.x to the InfoProvider. The InfoPackage can be enhanced by selection conditions that are used to extract just specific contents from the source system and update these in InfoCubes.

Types of InfoSources 3.x

The ETL (Extraction Transformation Loading) process illustrated in Figure 4.1 is dependent on the type of InfoSource 3.x. There are basically two InfoSource 3.x types:

- InfoSources with *direct* updating
- InfoSources with *flexible* updating

The preceding example is based on an InfoSource with flexible updating. InfoSources with flexible updating can also supply other InfoProviders with data at the same time. They are used primarily to update flow data in InfoCubes and ODS objects.

InfoSources with direct updating, on the other hand, are not linked with InfoCubes or ODS objects via update rules. They are used to update precisely one target object and are generally used to update master data in InfoObjects. The data flow runs in a similar way to the InfoSource with flexible updating, with the exception that there are no update rules. This is why the update rule in Figure 4.1 has (*) next to it.

The next section explains the 7.0 data flow concept from SAP NetWeaver BI.

4.1.2 7.0 Data Flow Concept

The data flow within the new 7.0 data flow concept is displayed in detail in Figure 4.2.

Like the figure displaying the 3.x data flow concept, Figure 4.2 is divided into two parts, displaying the source system in the lower part using an SAP source system as an example, and displaying the SAP NetWeaver BI system in the upper part.

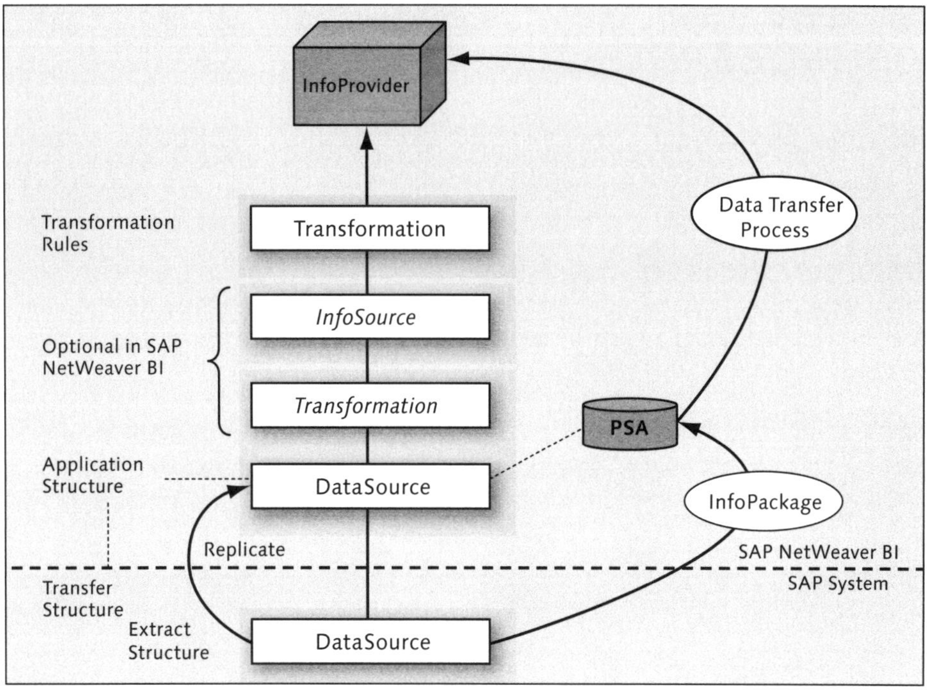

Figure 4.2 Data Flow Concept in SAP NetWeaver BI

DataSource

In SAP NetWeaver BI, the data flow always begins with a DataSource too. When you use Service API (SAPI), which contains the programs for extracting data from SAP source systems, you still have the special feature that allows the DataSource to be created directly in the source system.

Structures

The DataSource is made up of the extraction structure, which contains the field catalog of the fields to be extracted. In some applications, it does not make sense to transfer all of the fields from the source system to the SAP NetWeaver BI system, which is why fields of the extraction structure can be hidden. We call this subset of the fields the transfer structure, although this — unlike in SAP BW 3.x — is only referred to as such in the source system. After the DataSource has been replicated in SAP NetWeaver BI and then activated, the transfer structure is called the *application structure*, but it has the same meaning as in SAP BW.

Central DataSource Object

In contrast to the old data flow, the DataSource has replaced the transfer rule as the central object on which the persistent PSA can be found. After the DataSource has been replicated, you activate the DataSource, not the transfer rules. In doing so, the transfer structure is transferred from the source system, and the PSA is created based on the field structure of what is now the application structure.

The InfoSource is written in italics in Figure 4.2. In the new data flow, it has become an optional object; that is, you can leave it out. The transformation has replaced the related construction that comprised the transfer rule, InfoSource and update rule. As a result, we no longer differentiate between direct and flexible updating; rather we now just refer to (flexible) updating or transformation.

Transformation

The display format of the transformation has been revised, and new functions have been added (see Figure 4.3). In addition to the *start routine* for the transfer and update rules (with which we are already familiar) that accesses the source structure and can thus process data packages before the actual transformation, the end routine and expert routine have also been developed. The *end routine*, in contrast to the start routine, accesses the target structure; in other words, it accesses the data *after* the transformation. The *expert routine* replaces the automatic transformation; using this routine, the developer has to manually assign the data in ABAP objects within a method. When you choose the expert routine as the transformation, the start and end routines are no longer available. Furthermore, no monitor entries are written; the developer has to do these himself.

You can therefore link DataSources directly with InfoProviders, such as InfoCubes and DSO objects, as well as with InfoObjects. All types of updates or transfers have become transformations; a distinction is no longer made between the two forms.

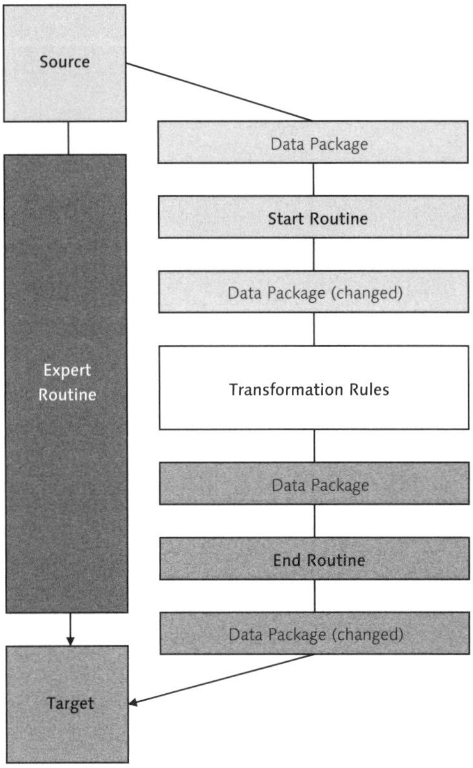

Figure 4.3 New Options within Transformation

InfoPackage and the Data Transfer Process

The InfoPackage, which in SAP BW 3.x is responsible for requesting data in the source system and then updating it in the data targets, is now only responsible for requesting data from the source system in SAP NetWeaver BI. The earlier options, which allowed data to be updated in the InfoProvider, are no longer available. They have been replaced by the *data transfer process* (DTP). Data transfer processes always accompany a transformation and connect persistent objects, in other words, objects that physically carry data. It is therefore necessary to give each transformation a DTP, which controls the updating process.

Although the DTP does not at first appear to be necessary, it has numerous advantages.

- **Save erroneous data records**
  Data packages that have errors do not automatically cause the update to terminate. The incorrect information is written to an error stack, which processes it and updates it after correction.
- **Clarity within the data flow**
  The DTP increases the clarity within the data flow, particularly if many temporary objects in the system are involved in the data flow.
- **Semantic groups**
  Depending on the criteria you define, data transfer processes can distinguish between data records that are to be named the same and ones that are not. We refer to "semantic groups" within the DTP here.
- **Enhanced filter conditions**
  You can specify filter conditions that contain each field of the source structure and were not just defined as selection parameters.

Other special features are described in the following section.

4.1.3 Differences Between the Two Concepts

This section summarizes the differences between the 3.x and the 7.0 data flow concepts and lists the special features for migration.

- **Transformation replaces transfer and update rules**
  The various rules available in SAP BW 3.x for data transformation (transfer rules, update rules) have been replaced by transformation, which can be modeled easily using graphical assignment.
- **Start, end, and expert routines in the transformation**
  The start routine, which could be used in transfer and update rules, has been enhanced by the end routine and the expert routine. The end routine accesses the target structure; using the expert routine, you can (and must) make all assignments with ABAP objects.
- **InfoSource as an optional object**
  The InfoSource is no longer a mandatory object. You can now decide if you want to use an InfoSource or not.
- **New object: Data transfer process**
  The data transfer process replaces the updating of data in the data targets by

InfoPackages. DTP accompanies transformations and updates data between persistent objects.

- **DataSource as a central object**
  The PSA is now attached to the DataSource and no longer to the transfer rule. When the DataSource is activated, all of the objects required for the data request are activated.
- **Displaying the entire data flow in the Data Warehousing Workbench**
  Besides being able to display the data flow graphically via the context menu, you can now also view it directly in the Data Warehousing Workbench (see Figure 4.4).

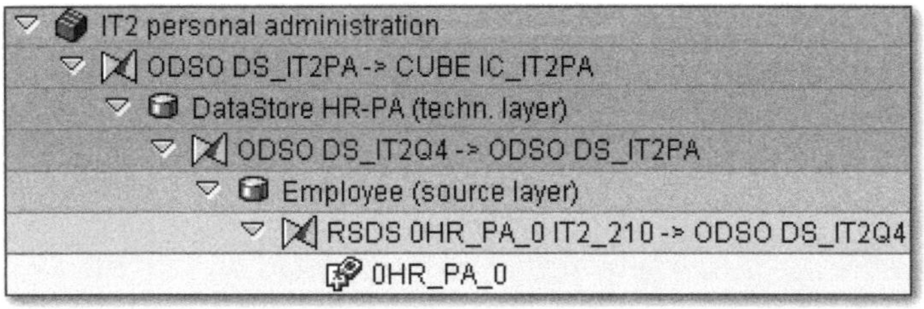

Figure 4.4 Displaying the Data Flow Within the Data Warehousing Workbench

- **DSO and InfoCube modeling alignment**
  You now model InfoCubes in the same way as DSO objects. The alignment has been carried over from the modeling of ODS objects in SAP BW 3.x.
- **Conversion from ABAP to ABAP objects**
  All source texts within SAP NetWeaver BI, whether they are start routines, end routines, or routines that make assignments within transformations from the source structure to the target structure, now have to be written in ABAP objects.

The migration of the data flow can, to a large extent, be carried out according to predefined rules and concepts. However, it is precisely the final point mentioned, the conversion from ABAP to ABAP objects as the underlying programming language, that very frequently hinders the migration. In addition to the related object orientation within transformations and the different syntax, the conversion is further complicated by the fact that object names have changed.

For you, this means that wherever you have used ABAP source text within the data flow, for example, in start routines, characteristic routines, or routines within update rules, you won't be able to get around making manual adjustments. Depending on the complexity of the source text, these are time-consuming aspects of the data flow migration.

What does not cause a problem, on the other hand, is the omission of the InfoSource as a mandatory object. You can continue to use the InfoSource and don't have to delete it. You simply have to migrate the transfer and update rules from and to the InfoSource in transformations.

Recommendation

In some cases, the InfoSource was a "necessary evil" because no changes had been made to the field contents from DataSource to InfoSource. To maintain a clear overview, you should delete the InfoSource in these instances.

You should also become familiar with the new concepts to get the most out of them. Make full use of the transfer processes, for example, and use the error stack. Take a look at the end routine and consider whether this might sometimes be more useful than the start routine.

4.2 Concept Migration Model

Now that you are familiar with the two data flow concepts from SAP BW 3.x and SAP NetWeaver BI, let's move on to the migration methods. Sections 4.3, Simple Migration Example, and 4.4, Complex Migration Example, present both a simple and a complex example of a migration, respectively.

Basic Rules

In this section, you'll work primarily with basic rules that should help you carry out the migration step by step. These rules are referred to again in the examples in Sections 4.3, Simple Migration Example, and 4.4, Complex Migration Example, to make it easier for you to follow the migration. The basic rules are identified by a gray box and are numbered.

As already mentioned in Section 2.1, Migrating the System Landscape, a migration always affects the entire system landscape; the concept migration is no exception to this. As a result, you always migrate the data flow on the development system and transport it to the production system after it has been tested successfully.

To prevent data loss and problems during migration, SAP has created a way of reversing the migration, but this only works up to a certain point, which will be noted in the example.

4.2.1 Old Data Flow Objects

After you have carried out the technical migration, you see your objects in Transaction RSA1 (Data Warehousing Workbench) in their familiar form, except that a small white box is displayed in front of each object (see Figure 4.5).

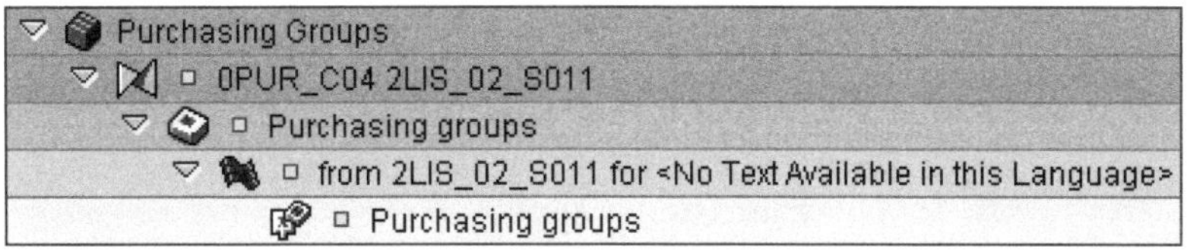

Figure 4.5 Old Data Flow in an SAP NetWeaver BI

The box means that a newer version exists for the specified objects. Because InfoCubes do not change in the data flow, the Purchasing Groups InfoCube shown in Figure 4.5 is not marked with a white box.

4.2.2 Data Flow Migration Concept

The most important rule to follow when migrating the data flow is the order in which you migrate the objects. Migrations are generally carried out top-down; in other words, they begin at the data target and end at the DataSource 3.x. This is, at the same time, the first basic rule.

Basic Rule 1: Sequence

The data flow migration is carried out top-down. It always begins at the data target and ends with the migration of the DataSource 3.x.

Accordingly, the objects are migrated in the following order for a data flow like the one shown in Figure 4.5:

1. Update rule (0PUR_C04 2LIS_02_S011)
2. InfoSource (Purchasing Groups)

3. Transfer rule (from 2LIS_02_S011 for IT2 Client 100)
4. DataSource (2LIS_02_S011)

Next, you need to consider whether the InfoSource in this data flow is really required or whether the data flow can be transferred directly from the DataSource to the InfoCube.

As mentioned at the start, it's generally possible to reverse a migration if, for example, you discover that problems have occurred with the new data flow. This, however, only applies under certain conditions, which leads to basic rule number two.

Basic Rule 2: Undo the Migration

In principle, you can undo the migration of the data flow provided that the DataSource has not yet been migrated. If you selected the WITH EXPORT option when migrating the DataSource, you can *always* restore the data flow to the old data flow.

The WITH EXPORT option for migrating the DataSource indicates whether you want to export the old structure information of the DataSource to the tables provided for this. The advantage of doing this is that you can restore a migration using Transaction RSDS if any errors occur. Selecting this option increases the migration time of the DataSource by approximately one to two minutes.

Note, however, that the old information exported from the DataSource is not transported. The migration can therefore only be restored on the development system and must then be transported.

In principle, the migration is an automated process, which is executed by the SAP NetWeaver BI system. Manual adjustments are only necessary if you have source text within routines or have made field assignments (see Section 4.4, Complex Migration Example). If, on the other hand, transfer and update rules are based on assignments only, the migration runs automatically.

Basic Rule 3: Automatic Migration

The data flow migration runs automatically. You'll only need to intervene manually at most when using your own ABAP source text within transfer and update rules.

You have already learned about the improvement to the new data flow, which means that we no longer differentiate between transfer and update and that we now simply talk about transformation. As a result, transfer rules and update rules always become transformations, as summarized in basic rule 4.

Basic Rule 4: Transformation

Transfer and update rules are migrated to a transformation. A distinction is no longer made between transfer and update rules.

In the following sections, you'll see how the basic rules apply in practice through the use of a simple and a complex example.

4.3 Simple Migration Example

This simple example uses the migration of the data flow to the Purchaser Group InfoCube, which has been copied one-to-one from the Business Content. The data flow from Figure 4.5 is shown in Figure 4.6 once again.

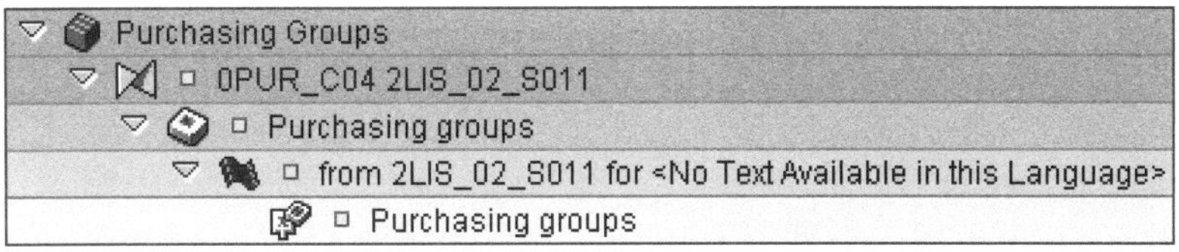

Figure 4.6 3.x Data Flow for the Purchasing Groups InfoCube

Note

Business Content is always available in the old 3.x data flow concept except in a small number of cases. When using Business Content, you must therefore also migrate the data flow in an SAP NetWeaver BI system!

The migration strictly follows basic rule 1. In this example, it therefore begins with the update rule and ends with the DataSource 3.x.

4.3.1 Migrating the Update Rule and the InfoSource 3.x

Before you start, look more closely at the update rule. The update rule is only migrated automatically if the update rule does not contain any routines you've programmed yourself (see basic rule 3). Although these routines are also transferred, you may have to correct them manually after the migration because of the conversion from ABAP to ABAP objects. The update rule in this example does not contain any code in the form of a start routine or routines for calculating key figures, as shown in Figure 4.7.

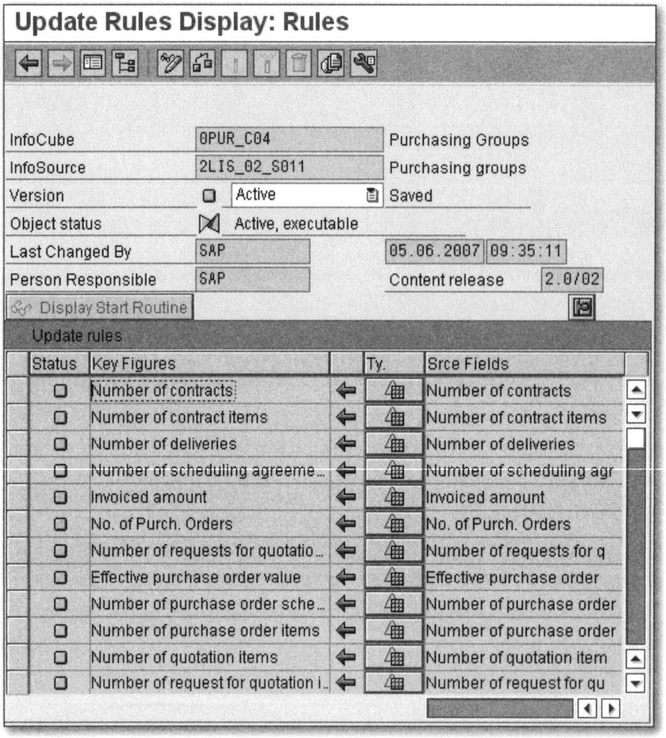

Figure 4.7 Update Rule for Purchasing Groups InfoCube

According to basic rule 4, the new data flow no longer contains any update rules; they become a transformation. You migrate the update rule to a transformation via the context menu for the update rule (ADDITIONAL FUNCTIONS • CREATE TRANSFORMATION), as shown in Figure 4.8.

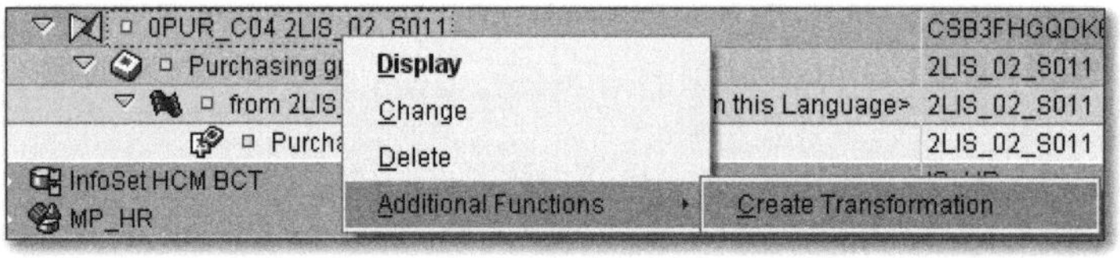

Figure 4.8 Creating the Transformation from the Update Rule

Basic rule 5, which is introduced later in Section 4.4.3, states that no objects are deleted during a migration; copies of the old objects are always created. This means that the undo function mentioned in basic rule 2 is also always available for the migration.

After the transformation has been created, the SAP NetWeaver BI system recognizes that it's an update rule, which is linked to an InfoSource 3.x. This is why the SAP NetWeaver BI system asks you whether you also want to migrate the InfoSource, to which you can answer yes (see Figure 4.9).

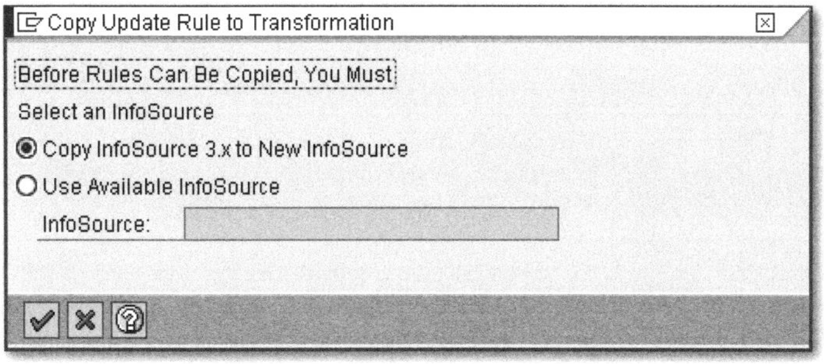

Figure 4.9 Creating a Copy of the InfoSource

Referring again to basic rule 5, the old InfoSource 3.x stays the same and is just copied; in other words, the old data flow remains untouched. In this example, the new InfoSource is given the technical name Y2LIS_02_S011 (see Figure 4.10).

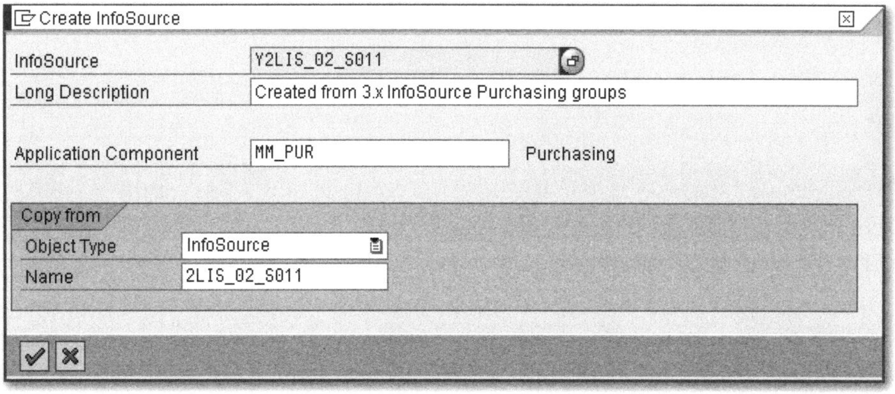

Figure 4.10 Creating the InfoSource as a Copy of the 3.x InfoSource

After you've specified the parameters, you can start the transformation process. A log is then displayed informing you that the transformation of the update rule and the InfoSource 3.x was successful (see Figure 4.11).

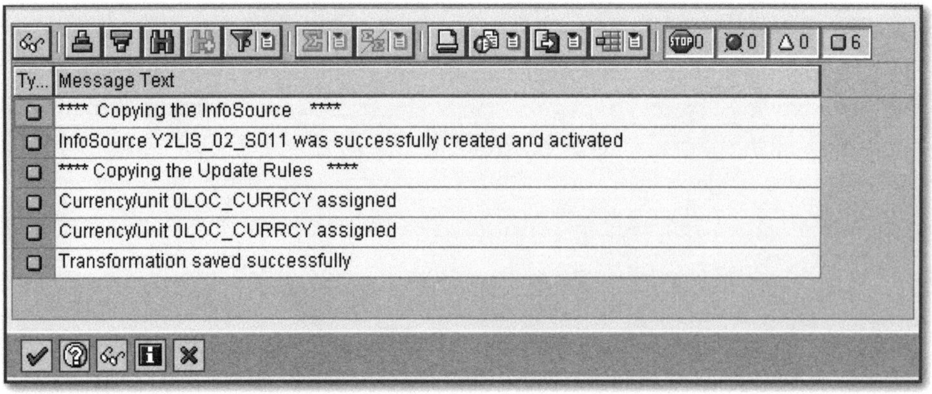

Figure 4.11 Migration Log for the Update Rule and the InfoSource 3.x

You can then see in the RSA1 that the data flow for the Purchasing Groups InfoCube has changed. You now have two InfoSources that supply the InfoCube with data. The InfoSource just created from the update rule is still inactive, as Figure 4.12 shows.

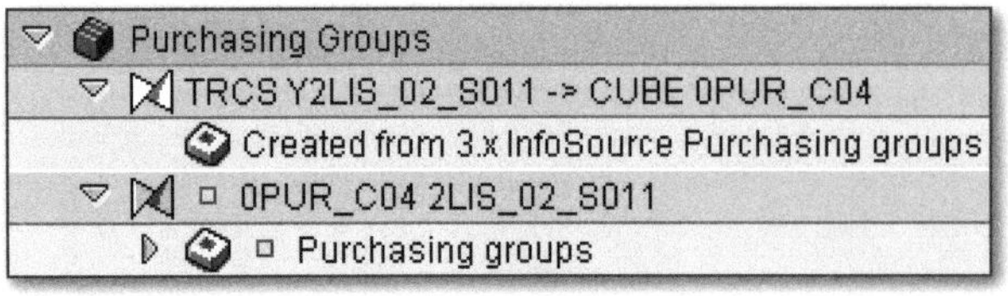

Figure 4.12 Data Flow after Migrating the Update Rule and InfoSource 3.x

A transformation is — even if it does not contain any ABAP code — never activated after it has been migrated successfully; its status is always inactive. You must now edit the transformation manually and activate it, provided this is possible (see Figure 4.13). You do this by performing a simple check of the transformation created. In this case, the check runs without errors, so it can be activated.

The data flow has now been migrated successfully up to the InfoSource. Next, you migrate the transfer rule.

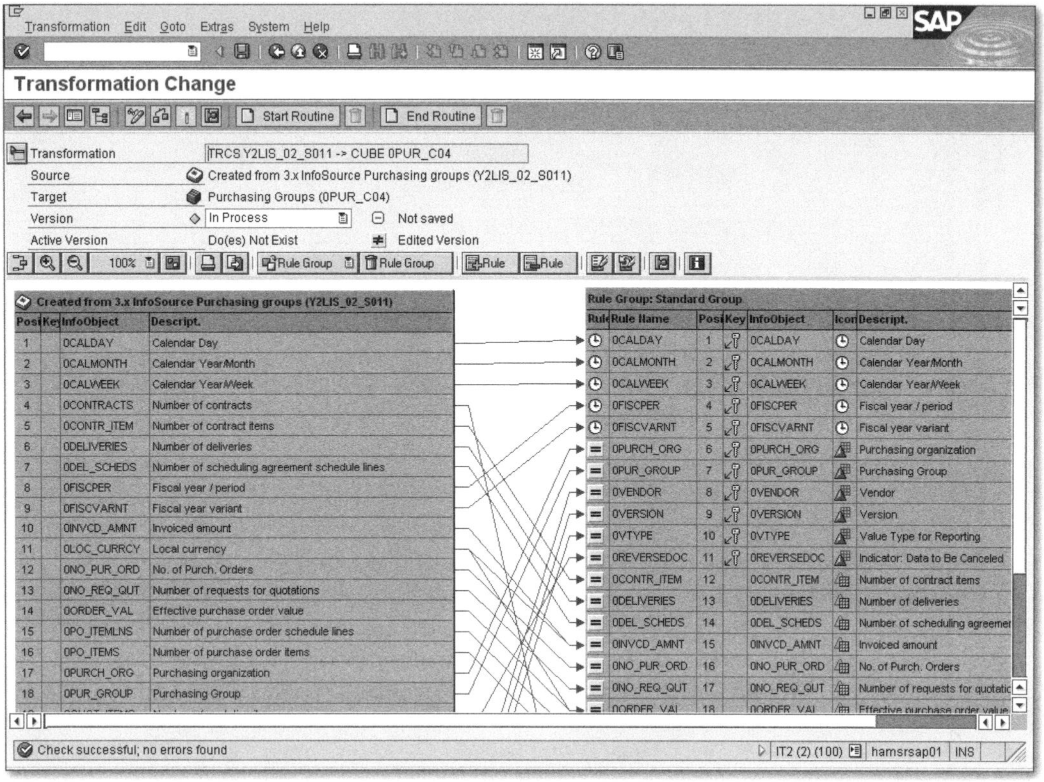

Figure 4.13 Editing and Checking the Transformation for Activation

4.3.2 Migrating the Transfer Rule

After you have successfully activated the transformation, you have a completely new data flow from a new InfoSource to the InfoCube 0PUR_C04. You then have to migrate the transfer rule. Here too, you should check first that no programming is contained, which must later be adjusted manually. Figure 4.14 shows you that this is not the case here.

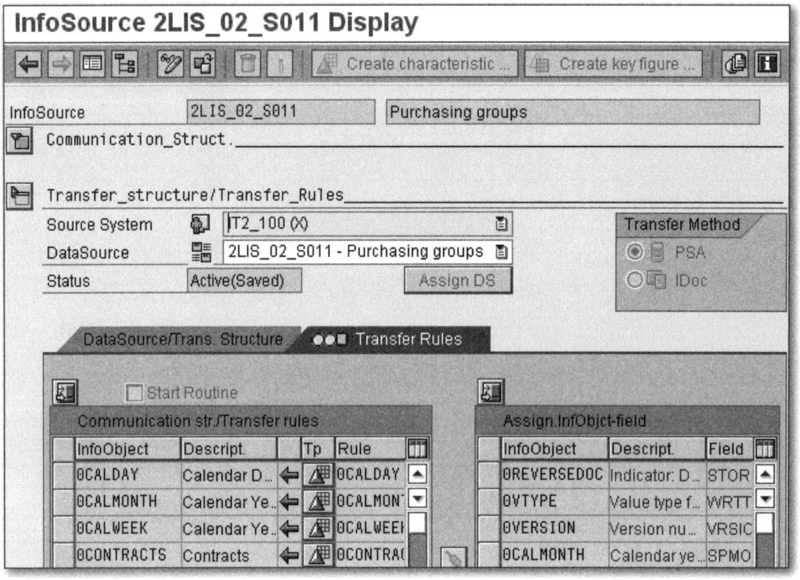

Figure 4.14 Checking the Transfer Rule for the Use of ABAP Source Text

A transfer rule also becomes a transformation here too (see basic rule 4). You therefore migrate the transfer rule in the same way as the update rule by choosing (ADDITIONAL FUNCTIONS • CREATE TRANSFORMATION) from the context menu, as Figure 4.15 shows.

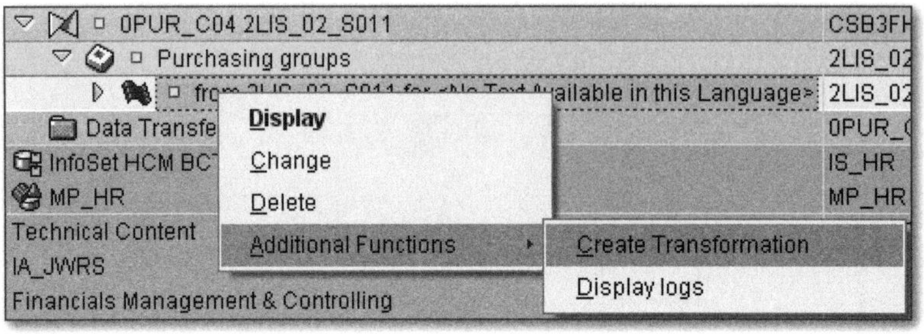

Figure 4.15 Creating the Transformation from the Transfer Rule

When migrating the transfer rule, the SAP NetWeaver BI system also asks you for which InfoSource you want to create the new transformation. Because you have already migrated the InfoSource 3.x in the previous step, you can specify the copied InfoSource in this step. The system will default to this InfoSource when it begins (see Figure 4.16).

Figure 4.16 Use of the New InfoSource for the Transformation to Be Created

A warning message "Automatic time conversion not possible for source field SPMON" is then displayed. You can confirm this message in this step. The system indicates to you that it is unable to perform the automatic time conversion from field SPMON to field 0CALMONTH because it does not recognize the data type of the field SPMON. You can correct the problem directly afterward in the transformation.

You receive this message again for other fields for which automatic time conversion is also not possible. When the migration is complete, a summary of activities for the migration is displayed in the application log (see Figure 4.17).

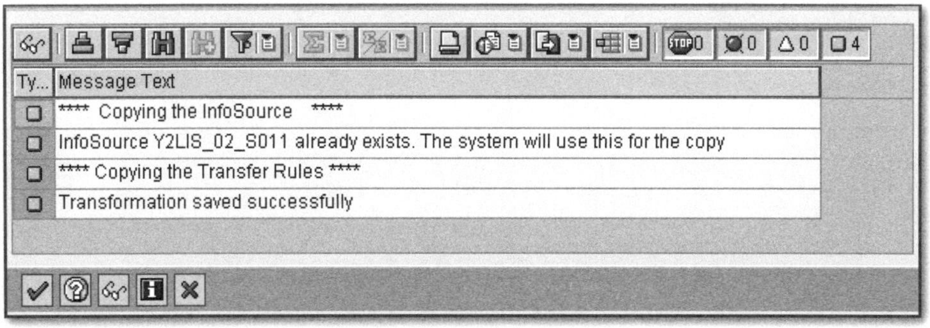

Figure 4.17 Application Log After Migrating the Transfer Rule

The new (inactive) transformation of the DataSource 3.x to the new InfoSource has now been added to the data flow, as is shown in Figure 4.18.

Figure 4.18 Enhanced New Data Flow Following the Migration

The display can be confusing at first because the transformation appears directly below the transfer rule. It will only be displayed correctly after the DataSource 3.x has been migrated.

You can now edit and check the transformation you have just created and then activate it (see Figure 4.19).

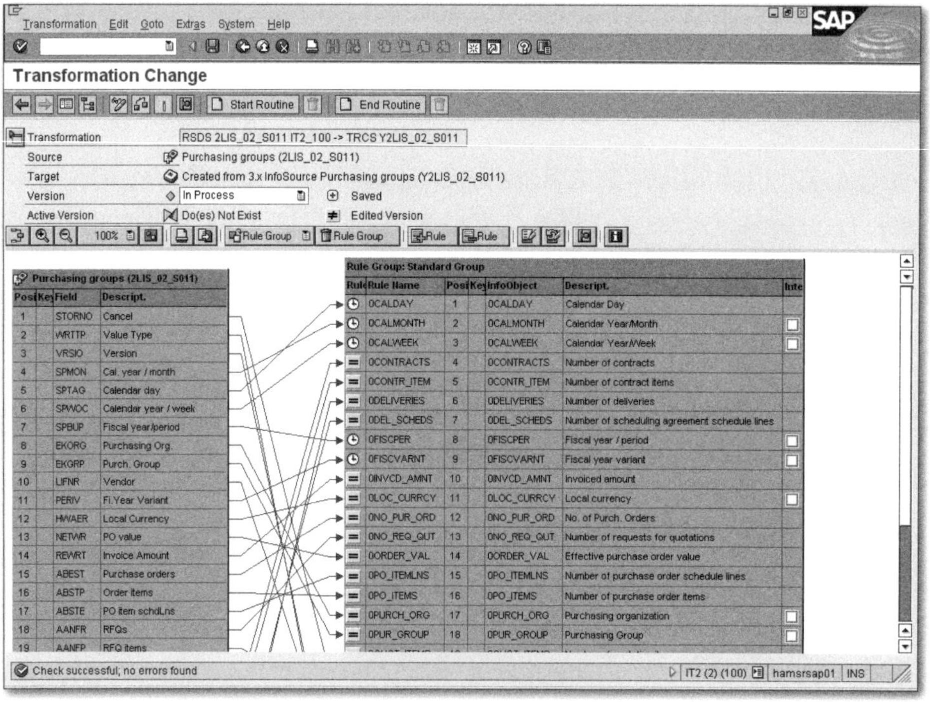

Figure 4.19 New Transformation of DataSource 3.x to InfoSource

Even though the transformation check ran successfully, you should still correct the warning message that appears when the transformation was created. This message informed you that an automatic time conversion was not possible; in other words, the system does not recognize that fields SPMON, SPTAG, and SPWOC have a time format. You can resolve this problem by assigning the InfoObjects 0CALMONTH, 0CALDAY, and 0CALWEEK to the three fields SPMON, SPTAG, and SPWOC. By doing this, you are explaining to the SAP NetWeaver BI system that this is the format in which the fields from the DataSource arrive. Figure 4.20 demonstrates this procedure using the SPTAG field as an example.

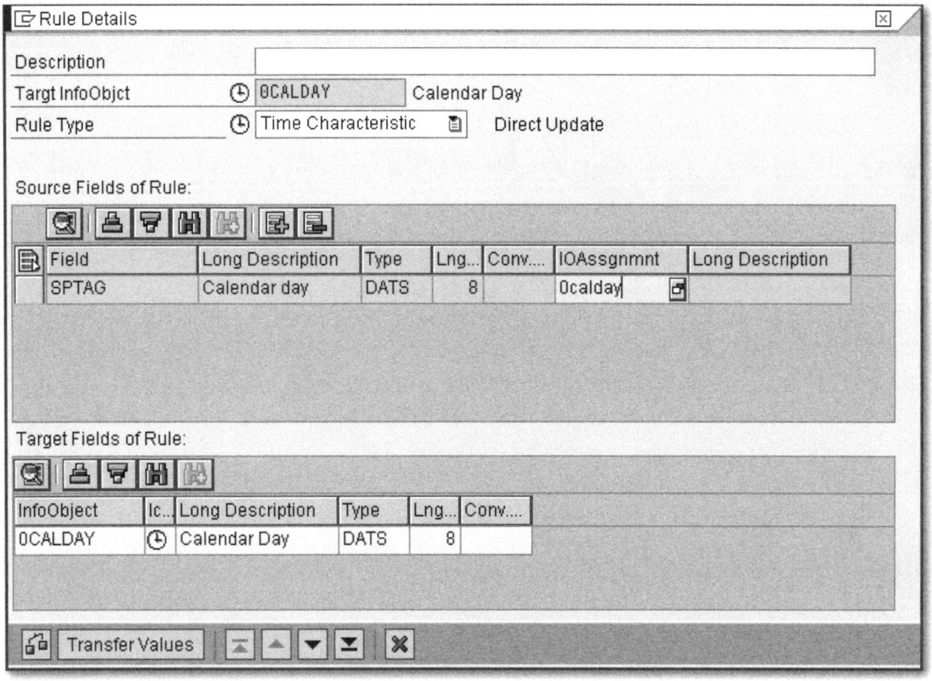

Figure 4.20 Assigning the InfoObjects 0CALDAY to the DataSource Field SPTAG

Do the same for the fields SPMON (InfoObject 0CALMONTH) and SPWOC (InfoObject 0CALWEEK). You can then activate the transformation.

4.3.3 Migrating the DataSource 3.x

SAP software provides a special case in the system for test purposes. You can currently load an InfoCube using two different data flows, the old one and the new one. To do this, you have to create data transfer processes for the new transformations. The system allows this interim solution until you can ensure that the new data flow is working correctly. Only then can you migrate the DataSource.

You also migrate the DataSource via the context menu. To do this, choose MIGRATE from the DataSource context menu (see Figure 4.21).

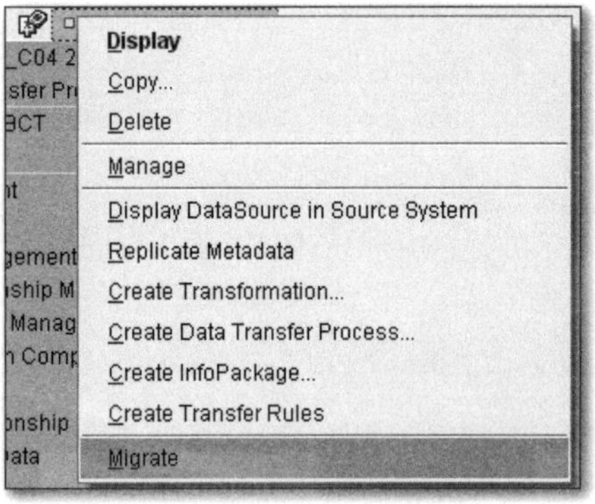

Figure 4.21 Migrating the DataSource 3.x via the Context Menu

Remember to always use the WITH EXPORT function for the migration (see basic rule 2); otherwise, the migration can no longer be undone (see Figure 4.22). You can then reverse the migration at any point using Transaction RSDS (CHOOSE DATASOURCE • RESTORE 3.X DS FROM THE MENU). The Info button in the window points this out to you once more.

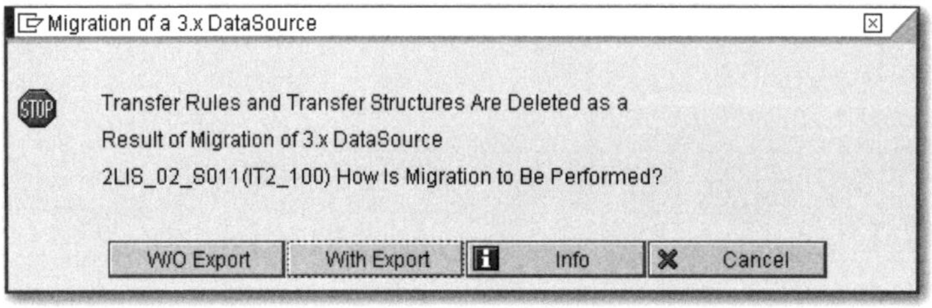

Figure 4.22 Migration Options for the 3.x DataSource

There is another special feature for the migration of the DataSource 3.x. In a standard migration, all objects in the system stay the same, and just copies are created. For the migration of the DataSource 3.x, however, the transfer rules are deleted and can only be restored again by Transaction RSDS (provided you selected the migration option WITH EXPORT).

When you choose the WITH EXPORT option, the migration takes about two to three minutes. The migration of the 3.x data flow is then completed. You have successfully migrated all of the objects involved in the data flow. The system then displays a screen in the RSA1, similar to that in Figure 4.23.

Figure 4.23 New Data Flow After the Migration

The migration is thus concluded. As a final step, you can now delete the InfoSource 3.x objects and the update rule, provided the test for the new data flow has run successfully.

To now use the data flow, you have to create a data flow process for the persistent objects DataSource and InfoCube (see Figure 4.24).

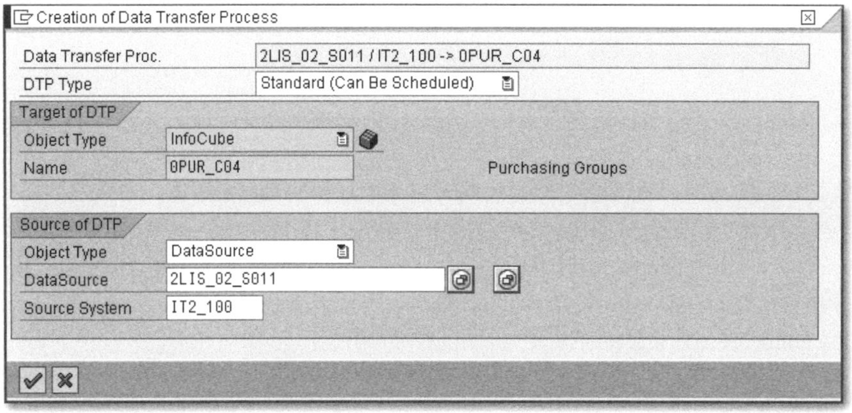

Figure 4.24 Creating a Data Transfer Process via the Context Menu

4.3.4 Conclusion

This simple example was intended to show you that a migration does not normally require manual intervention, provided you haven't used source text of your own. However, because you are often required to do so, the next example explains how to approach migration for complex data flows.

4.4 Complex Migration Example

The complex example is intended to show you where the limits of automatic migration are. This is the case if you have used ABAP code within transfer and update rules that cannot be copied one-to-one. After the transfer or update rule has been successfully migrated, it cannot be activated. Syntax errors in the transformation frequently cause this problem, which requires manual intervention on your part.

Caution

SAP NetWeaver BI systems mostly contain solutions that have been adapted to suit individual customers and are in themselves very different. This chapter, therefore, only points out possible causes of errors and provides you with general tips on how to perform the migration.

The example presented here comes from the area of Human Capital Management (HCM). Like the simple example, it comprises a DataSource 3.x, an InfoSource 3.x, and an InfoCube, which are all linked to each other via transfer and update rules.

4.4.1 Introducing the Example

The example loads the infotype 0008 (basic pay for employees) in a corresponding InfoCube in the SAP BW system. The infotype has a repetitive structure, which is why it can be typically used in a start routine (or alternatively a DataSource that is implemented via a function module). However, to keep things as simple as possible, we'll leave the description of the DataSource in the source system out because it isn't relevant for the migration. You can consider this to be a "black box."

A repetitive structure contains a large number of field names that are all the same except for their end digits, for example, ABC01, ABC02, ..., ABC50. Infotype 0008 contains the fields LGA01 to LGA40 and BET01 to BET40, where LGA stands for wage type and BET for amount.

In this way, you can assign 40 different wage types and their amounts to an employee, which are stored in just one data record of a table. This is efficient data storage for a transactional system such as the SAP HCM system. It does, however, complicate the evaluation of the data in an SAP BW system enormously. It doesn't make sense, for example, to create *one* InfoObject for each wage types field in infotype 0008 because the field has no meaning. Consequently, the wage type 1000 can be assigned to an employee with the personnel number 4711 in field LGA01; however, an employee with the personnel number 4712 is assigned the wage type 1000 in field LGA02. This means that you can never evaluate all of the amounts for wage type 1000 because all 40 InfoObjects must be included.

Therefore, you should transpose the repetitive structure; in other words, instead of creating 40 fields in one data record in an extreme case, create one field in 40 data records (see Figure 4.25).

Data Record from Infotype0008

PERNR	BEGDA	ENDDA	LGA01	BET01	LGA02	BET02	LGA03	BET03	...
4711	01/01/2007	12/31/9999	1001	4,502.17	1002	511.13	4000	30.00	...

Key Fields

Start Routine

Transformed Data Record

PERNR	BEGDA	ENDDA	LGART	BETRG
4711	01/01/2007	12/31/9999	1001	4,502.17
4711	01/01/2007	12/31/9999	1002	511.13
4711	01/01/2007	12/31/9999	4000	30.00
...	...	...	...	...

Key Fields

Figure 4.25 Transposing the Repetitive Structure

In the example, the three wage types 1001, 1002, and 4000 are assigned to employee 4711. These are contained in a data record in the format from infotype 0008 and are now transformed so that a data record is created for each wage type, which is then transferred to the InfoCube. By doing this, the preceding evaluation of all amounts can be carried out for the wage type 1000.

There are (at least) two variants for the conversion. With the first variant, you can develop your own extractor, which transforms the data and supplies it to the SAP BW system. The second variant transforms the data within a start routine in the transfer rule, as we've done here.

The conversion of the 3.x data flow in the SAP BW system is shown in Figure 4.26.

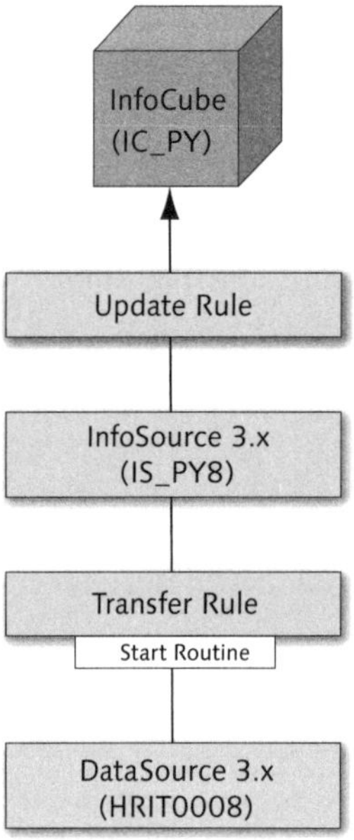

Figure 4.26 3.x Data Flow for the Complex Example

The technical name of the DataSource that extracts the data from infotype 0008 is HRIT0008. It's linked to the InfoSource with the technical name IS_PY8 via a transfer rule with a start routine. This, in turn, updates the data in the InfoCube IC_PY. The data is updated by an InfoPackage. Figure 4.27 illustrates the entire data flow within the migrated SAP BW system.

Figure 4.27 Data Flow Within the SAP BW System

You can see that the data flow is still in the 3.x format and must be migrated.

The DataSource from infotype 0008 provides you with the following fields:

- PERNR (Personnel Number)
- SPRPS (Lock Indicator)

- ENDDA (Valid To Date)
- BEGDA (Valid From Date)
- TRFAR (Pay Scale Type)
- TRFGB (Pay Scale Area)
- TRFGR (Pay Scale Group)
- TRFST (Pay Scale Level)
- WAERS (Currency Key)
- BSGRD (Capacity Utilization Level)
- LGA01 (Wage Type 01)
- BET01 (Amount 01)
- LGA02 (Wage Type 02) to LGA39 (Wage Type 39)
- BET02 (Amount 02) to BET39 (Amount 39)
- LGA40 (Wage Type 40)
- BET40 (Amount 40)

In this example, the DataSource extracts the forty wage types and amounts from infotype 0008. Besides transposing the repetitive structure, the remaining fields should be updated one-to-one in the InfoCube. This produces the following structure for the InfoSource:

- 0CALMONTH (Calendar Month)
- 0EMPLOYEE (Employee)
- 0PAYSCALEAR (Pay Scale Area)
- 0COUNTRY_ID (Country Grouping)
- 0PAYSCALETY (Pay Scale Type)
- 0PAYSCALEGR (Pay Scale Group)
- 0ESGFORCAP (Employee Subgroup Grouping for Collective Agreement Provision)
- 0PAYSCALELV (Pay Scale Level)
- 0PAYPCT_CHA (Capacity Utilization Level in %)
- 0CURRENCY (Currency)

- 0AMOUNT (Amount)
- 0WAGETYPE (Wage Type)

This includes all fields that originate from the DataSource.

The InfoCube includes one field more than the InfoSource (FTE), whose content can be calculated from the capacity utilization level. Another ABAP Routine is used here, which may later have to be adjusted manually. The dimensions of the InfoCube are shown in Figure 4.28.

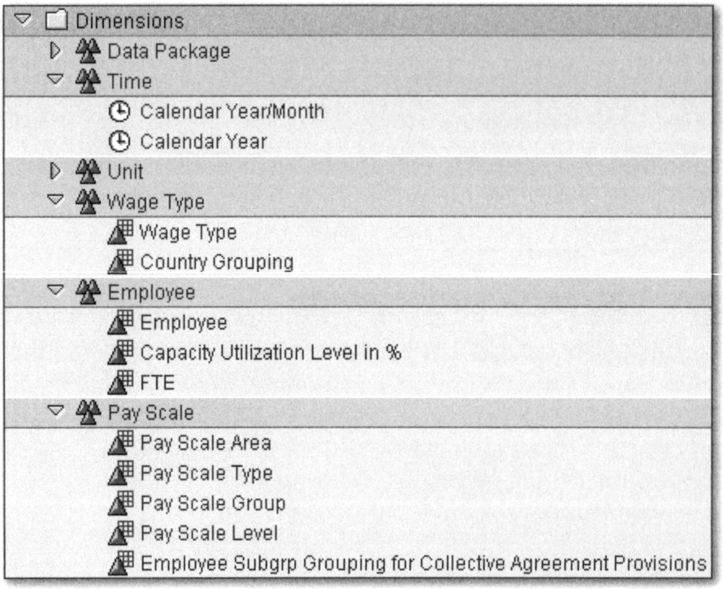

Figure 4.28 Dimensions of the InfoCube IC_PY from the Complex Example

4.4.2 Start Routine

The transformation of the repetitive structure is now performed by the start routine. It transforms fields LGA01 to LGA40 (or BET01 to BET40) so that the relevant information can always be found in LGA01 and BET01. This increases the number of data records in the data package. In other words, from one data record with wage type and amount information, a maximum of forty data records can be created, whose information exists in LGA01 and BET01 (refer to Figure 4.25).

The source text of the start routine is displayed in Listing 4.1. The transformation begins with a `LOOP` statement for each data package. To avoid producing forty paragraphs with (almost) identical source text, the start routine has been developed with field symbols. (Alternatively, you could also use a `DO...VARYING` loop.)

What is important is the termination condition at the end of the loop. By continually adding new data records, the data package grows and grows. In other words, the `LOOP` statement would never end. As a result, statements are only executed if one of the fields LGA02 to LGA40 is still filled. At the end, all of the information is in data record LGA01, and the loop can terminate.

```
DATA:
 l_s_datapak_line      TYPE transfer_structure,
 l_s_datapak_line_new TYPE transfer_structure,
 l_s_errorlog          TYPE rssm_s_errorlog_int,
 lv_index              TYPE i,
 lv_do_index           TYPE i,
 lv_str_index          TYPE string,
 lv_lgart              TYPE fieldname,
 lv_betrg              TYPE fieldname.
FIELD-SYMBOLS:
 <fs_betrg>            TYPE ANY,
 <fs_lgart>            TYPE ANY.

LOOP AT datapak INTO l_s_datapak_line.
 lv_index = sy-tabix.

* Delete locked employee
 IF l_s_datapak_line-sprps = 'X'.
  DELETE datapak INDEX lv_index.

* Only write wage types in the first field
* and create new record
 ELSE.
  IF l_s_datapak_line-lga02 IS NOT INITIAL.

      CLEAR l_s_datapak_line_new.
      MOVE-CORRESPONDING l_s_datapak_line
        TO l_s_datapak_line_new.
      CLEAR l_s_datapak_line_new-lga02.
      [...]
      CLEAR l_s_datapak_line_new-lga40.
```

```
    DO 40 TIMES.
     lv_do_index = sy-index.
     lv_str_index = lv_do_index.

* If smaller than 10 -> 0
     IF lv_do_index < 10.
      CONCATENATE '0' lv_str_index
        INTO lv_str_index.
     ENDIF.
     CONDENSE lv_str_index NO-GAPS.

* Create field names
     CONCATENATE 'LGA' lv_str_index
       INTO lv_lgart.
     CONDENSE lv_lgart NO-GAPS.
     CONCATENATE 'BET' lv_str_index
       INTO lv_betrg.
     CONDENSE lv_betrg NO-GAPS.

* Assignment from source structure
     ASSIGN COMPONENT lv_lgart OF STRUCTURE
       l_s_datapak_line TO <fs_lgart>.
     ASSIGN COMPONENT lv_betrg OF STRUCTURE
       l_s_datapak_line TO <fs_betrg>.

* Fill LGA01/BET01 "target structure"
     IF <fs_betrg> IS NOT INITIAL.
      l_s_datapak_line_new-lga01 = <fs_lgart>.
      l_s_datapak_line_new-bet01 = <fs_betrg>.
      APPEND l_s_datapak_line_new TO datapak.
     ENDIF.
    ENDDO.

* Delete current record (termination condition!)
    DELETE datapak INDEX lv_index.
   ENDIF.
 ENDIF.
ENDLOOP. " at datapak into l_s_datapak_line

* abort <> 0 means skip whole data package!!!
ABORT = 0.
```

Listing 4.1 Source Text of the Start Routine

This start routine consists of just the section in which you may add source text yourself. The start routine itself is a program called CONVERSION_ROUTINE. In SAP NetWeaver BI, the procedure has changed; the program has become a method. This also changes key field names, such as DATAPAK and the data type TRANSFER_STRUCTURE. Later in this section, you'll see what happens to these field names during the migration.

4.4.3 Migration

In the complex example, the migration is also carried out according to basic rule 1, which means that it starts with the update rule. Although we expect the migration to run successfully, we can't activate the transformation because it contains our own source text. The transformation contains a routine that assigns the capacity utilization level to the FTE field divided by 100 (see Listing 4.2).

```
* result value of the routine
  data: lv_fte type /bi0/oipaypct,
        lv_fte_c(10) type c.

  lv_fte = COMM_STRUCTURE-paypct_cha / 100.
  lv_fte_c = lv_fte.

  RESULT = lv_fte_c.

* if the returncode is not equal to zero, the
* result will not be updated
  RETURNCODE = 0.

* if abort is not equal to zero, the update
* process will be canceled
  ABORT = 0.
```

Listing 4.2 Creating the FTE Field Information as the Capacity Utilization Level Divided by 100

You start the migration by right-clicking the update rule and choosing ADDITIONAL FUNCTIONS • CREATE TRANSFORMATION from the context menu. You are asked to decide what should happen with the connected InfoSource 3.x (IS_PY8). We will migrate it in the same step, as we did in the simple example (see Figure 4.29).

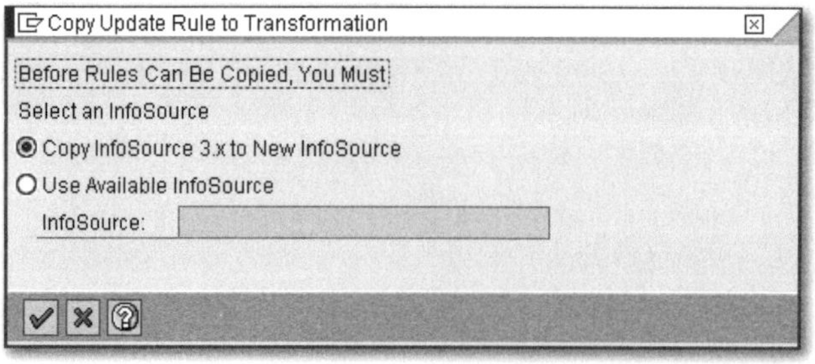

Figure 4.29 Creating a New InfoSource Based on the 3.x InfoSource

You can then give the DataSource a new name. In this case, we place a Z in front of the technical name and create ZIS_PY8 as the new DataSource (see Figure 4.30).

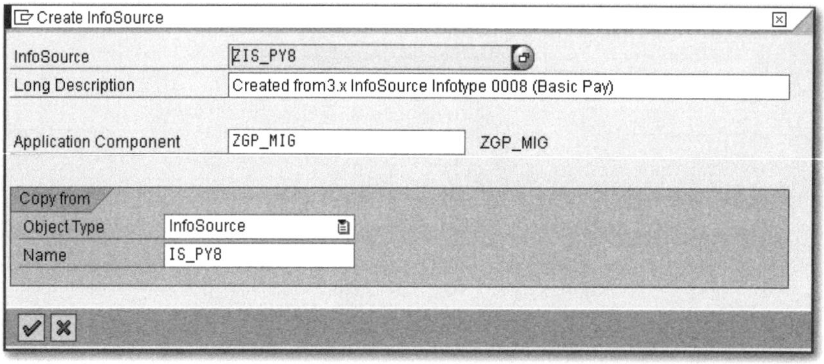

Figure 4.30 Creating the New InfoSource ZIS_PY8

The migration for the update rule and the InfoSource 3.x then begins. It concludes with the migration log with which you are already familiar. In this case, a warning message is displayed, which relates to the specific routine for the FTE (ANZFTE) characteristic (see Figure 4.31). The message advises you to check the syntax for the routine.

The transformation has now been created, but its status is still inactive. The subsequent syntax check in the transformation now even runs without errors.

Why is this? Because this behavior will also occur for the start routine, the answer to this will be provided later in this section, when we'll be dealing with the situation after migrating the transfer rule.

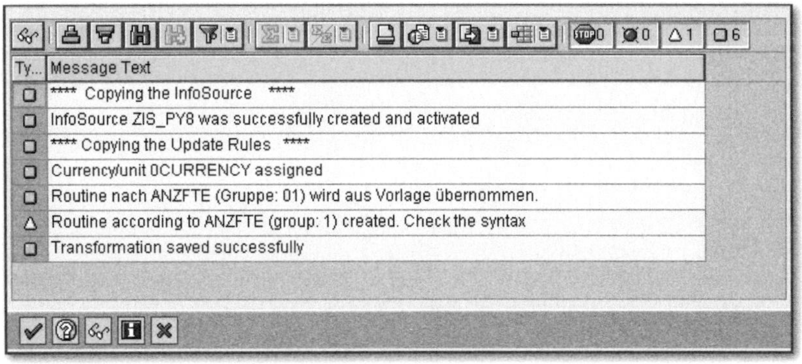

Figure 4.31 Log for the Migration of the Update Rule and InfoSource 3.x

After the syntax has been checked successfully, you can activate the transformation. Your data flow up to the InfoSource should resemble the one shown in Figure 4.32.

Figure 4.32 Data Flow After Migrating the Update Rule and InfoSource 3.x

Next, you migrate the transfer rule via the context menu for the transfer rule (ADDITIONAL FUNCTIONS • CREATE TRANSFORMATION). Do not create a new InfoSource now. Instead, select the InfoSource ZIS_PY8, which you created in the previous step. The subsequent log informs you again that the InfoSource was copied successfully (see Figure 4.33).

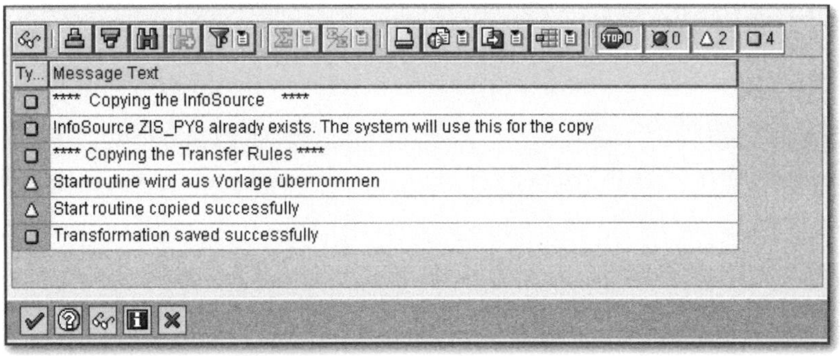

Figure 4.33 Log for the Migration of the Transfer Rule

As mentioned earlier, the syntax check for the transformation created from the transfer rule ran without errors, which is an unexpected result.

The concepts from the 3.x and 7.0 data flow have changed fundamentally; that is, the program for the start routine has become a method. Here too, all parameter names have changed, as mentioned earlier.

The SAP migration program, which is used for migrating the update and transfer rules, adds the old program for the start routine to the new method and transfers the new parameters to the old ones (see Figure 4.34). In doing this, field names do not have to change from their old transformation, and the transformation can still run automatically, provided that the source texts do not have to be converted.

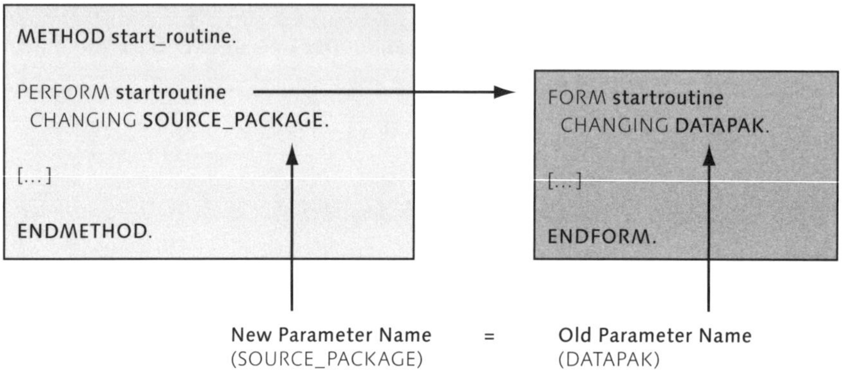

Figure 4.34 Calling the Old Start Routine from the New Routine

Transfer and update rule migrations therefore run automatically; they only require manual intervention if obsolete ABAP constructions are used. These aspects are summarized for you in the following basic rules:

Basic Rule 5: Migrating Update Rules and Transfer Rules

Update and transfer rules, which contain ABAP source code within field assignments or start routines, must generally be adjusted manually because the SAP migration program transfers new field names to the old ones. Adjustments are only necessary if obsolete ABAP statements were used, which are no longer allowed in the course of ABAP objects.

Many developers shy away from converting their ABAP statements to ABAP objects because this can be a time-consuming process. If, to begin with, you just want to restore the functionality following the migration, then it's also possible to use an interim solution. Move the source text from the start routine to a function module, and call this from the migrated routine. This allows you to continue working with ABAP in the function module without having to take the — actually useful — syntax restrictions in ABAP objects into account. However, you should only use this as a temporary measure to ensure the initial operation.

You can now migrate the DataSource 3.x by choosing Migrate (migration WITH EXPORT) from the context menu of DataSource HRIT0008. The entire data flow is then available to you, as Figure 4.35 shows. You now just have to create a data transfer process, and you can then test the migration.

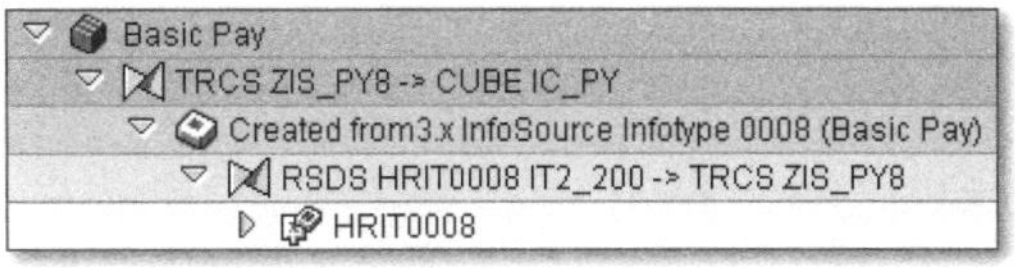

Figure 4.35 Data Flow After Successful Migration

4.4.4 Conclusion

The only exception for migrating the data flow occurs in the transfer of the ABAP syntax to the ABAP objects syntax. There is no automatic program here to take the work off your hands. However, the syntax check within the transformations does indicate to you the areas that need editing. You can then use the F1 Help at the points the errors occurred to find out what construction has taken their place.

4.5 Recommendations for the Migration Project

To conclude this chapter, let's talk about the project costs now that you have seen how the data flow is migrated.

4.5.1 Cost Considerations

Migrating the data flow is a largely automated process, in which you only have to intervene manually if you have developed your own source text that is no longer compatible with ABAP objects. This does *not* mean that you now have to implement your function module-based logic in classes. Rather, the aim is to replace language constructs that were allowed in ABAP but which are now obsolete in ABAP objects with new constructs that are ABAP object.

Example

In ABAP, it was possible to use internal tables without header lines. ABAP objects no longer allow this syntax, which means that source texts of the following type are obsolete:

```
DATA: lt_table TYPE TABLE OF tabl.

CLEAR lt_table.
lt_table-feld = '123'.
APPEND lt_table.
```

You have to replace this construction with the following:

```
DATA: lt_table TYPE TABLE OF tabl,
      ls_table LIKE LINE OF lt_table.

CLEAR ls_table.
ls_table-feld = '123'.
APPEND ls_table to lt_table.
```

The cost of migrating the data flow is thus considered to be relatively small, in particular when you compare this with migrating the web reporting. Furthermore, you can also temporarily resort to the variant that allows you to move the source text of your routines to function modules and to call this in the migrated routines.

Depending on the complexity of your data model, however, this migration can also drag out and take weeks. As a guide, you can estimate about one hour (although this can vary for very complex routines) for the pure migration of a simple data flow (1 InfoCube, 1 InfoSource, 1 DataSource), including a short test. For each persistent object (e.g., InfoCube, ODS object) you add, you can calculate a further half hour.

To estimate the costs, you can create an Excel table from one of the data flows. To do this, look at the data flow in the Data Warehousing Workbench by clicking DISPLAY DATA FLOW in the context menu of an InfoProvider. This displays a graphical view of the data flow for the InfoProvider. Either transfer the list to an Excel table, or add the costs directly to the graphic.

The migration of our simple example and of our complex example would each take one hour. This time was not completely used up because the source text was already ABAP object-compliant. Other examples, on the other hand, could be more complex and may take more than one hour.

Note, too, that selection conditions in InfoPackages now only apply for the extraction up to the PSA. If you want to make selections beyond this, you have to develop new filter criteria in the related data transfer processes. This can also take time. Furthermore, your process chains change to the effect that you have to insert data transfer processes.

4.5.2 Recommendation

You should migrate the data flow because the new functions certainly justify the relatively low costs of the migration. Note, however, that changes to the data flow can also bring about changes to other applications too, such as process chains. In addition to the pure migration costs, additional costs can also arise if you want to use new concepts, such as error stacks, and so on, which were not previously possible.

4.6 Summary

In this chapter, you have learned about migrating the data flow. The beginning of the chapter covered the structures of the data flows in SAP BW and SAP NetWeaver BI and the differences between these. This knowledge is essential for carrying out the migration.

The chapter then detailed the migration process for you. You also learned about the SAP migration procedure and witnessed what problems can arise and where. The main objective of converting the data flow lies in the transformation of ABAP to ABAP objects.

You saw the principle applied in both a simple and a complex example as a complete migration was carried out in each case. Finally, you now know the costs involved in this migration and how you can calculate these costs.

5 Migrating Authorizations

This chapter shows you how to migrate from the old authorization concept to the new one. As in the previous chapter, you'll first get an introduction to the authorization concepts of SAP BW and SAP NetWeaver BI and see the differences between them. Then, the migration principle will be explained, followed by an example. The chapter will be rounded out with some notes about the effort required to migrate from the old to new concept.

5.1 Authorization Concepts

The introduction of the analysis authorization has significantly changed the authorization concepts of SAP BW and SAP NetWeaver BI. So, we'll start by discussing the new concept and then highlight how it differs from the old authorization concept.

In SAP NetWeaver BI, *analysis authorizations* are responsible for reporting. This type of authorization differs from the classic SAP authorization concept and is created and managed with the new Transaction RSECADMIN. You can use analysis authorizations to assign authorizations in reporting at various levels:

- **Authorization at the InfoCube level**
  Here you limit the authorization to individual InfoCubes. Users have full authorization or no authorization at all for a given InfoCube.
- **Authorization at the characteristic level**
  As is the case with assigning authorizations for InfoCubes, you can assign authorizations for individual characteristics. Accordingly, reporting users can use the characteristic completely or not at all.
- **Authorization at the characteristic value level**
  This authorization controls individual characteristic attributes, so the level is used often. With this authorization, you can limit users to individual values or sets of values, such as to individual company codes, organizational units, or material groups.

- **Authorization at the key figure level**
  When you assign authorizations for key figures, you can prohibit access to individual key figures.
- **Authorization to the hierarchy node level**
  An additional level assigns authorizations for hierarchies. Here you have an option to assign authorizations to subtrees or individual nodes that you can also define in relation to other nodes. You can also assign authorizations at the leaf level in a hierarchy.

All properties of analysis authorizations can be combined with each other. Nevertheless, an analysis authorization functions are different from what you might expect:

- When accessing data that corresponds to a subset of the authorized data (successful authorization check), you see the data according to your selection (see Figure 5.1).

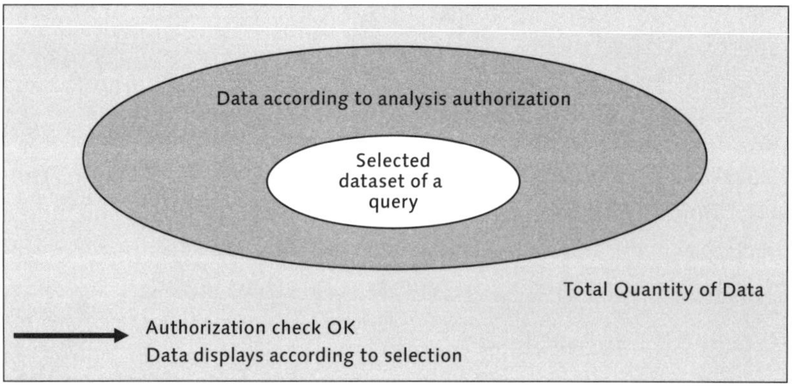

Figure 5.1 Successful Authorization Check — Data Is Displayed

- If you attempt to access data that is not covered by your authorization, you don't see the subset for which you actually do have authorization. You simply receive a message: "No authorization" (see Figure 5.2).

Authorizations for hierarchies and key figures are exceptions to this rule. If you have authorizations for specific hierarchy nodes, the data of the hierarchy for which you have authorization is displayed when you include the hierarchy. The situation is similar for key figures in that you see the key figures for which you have authorization.

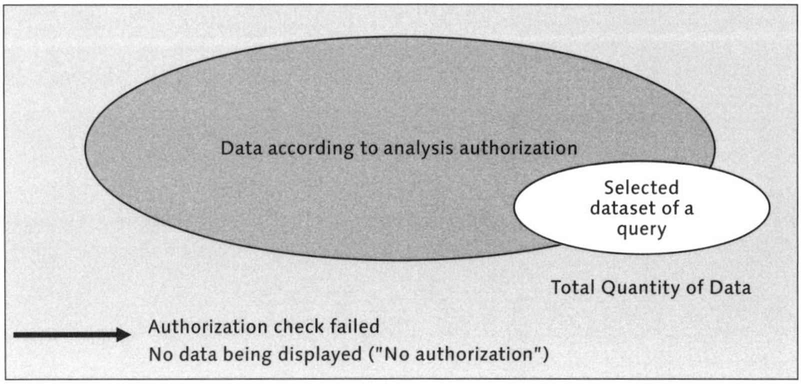

Figure 5.2 Unsuccessful Authorization Check — No Data Is Displayed

5.1.1 Setting Up Analysis Authorizations

You can assign analysis authorizations only for InfoObjects that you have flagged as relevant to authorizations. You make the setting for an InfoObject with Transaction RSD1 in the BUSINESS EXPLORER tab. These InfoObjects are then available to you for use in analysis authorizations.

You can create analysis authorizations using Transaction RSECADMIN (see Figure 5.3). They are managed in the Authorizations tab with the maintenance function.

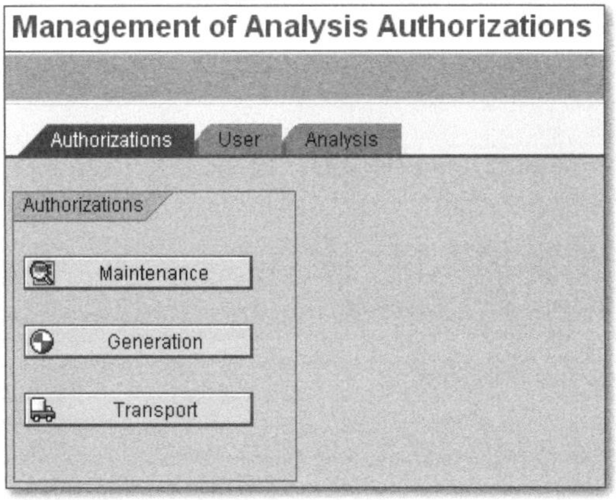

Figure 5.3 Initial Screen of Transaction RSECADMIN to Manage Analysis Authorizations

After you select the maintenance function, you can either open an existing authorization or create a new one. To create a new one, enter a technical name, and select CREATE (see Figure 5.4).

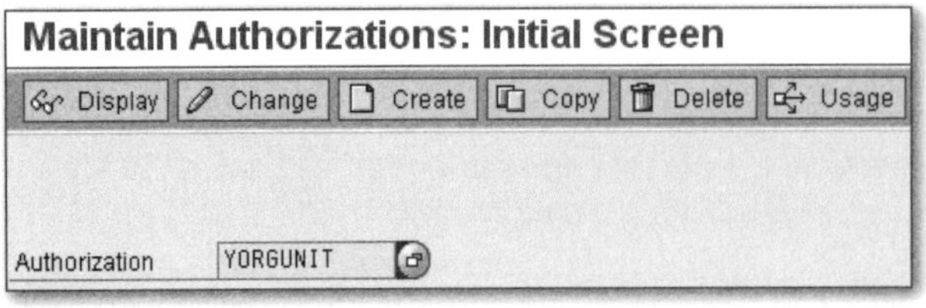

Figure 5.4 Creating a New Analysis Authorization

You then see a screen that you can use to define the authorization structure. All of the options noted at the beginning of this section are available to you here. You can assign authorizations for characteristics, characteristic values, InfoCubes, hierarchies, or key figures (see Figure 5.5).

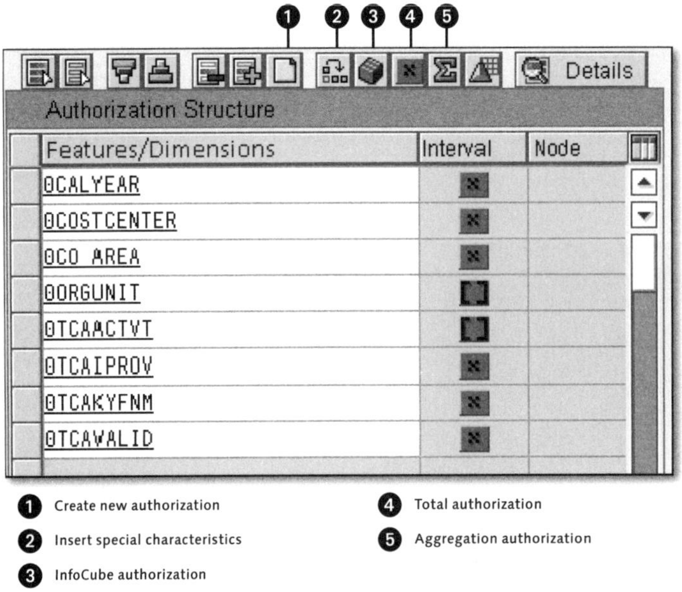

Figure 5.5 Assigning Authorizations with Transaction RSECADMIN

The sample analysis authorization, YORGUNIT, consists of eight different characteristics. The first four characteristics were created with GENERATE NEW AUTHORIZATION: they are limitations for specific characteristics and characteristic values.

The asterisk (*) in the INTERVALS column means that the analysis authorization assigned a full authorization for the characteristic. For example, you can assign a full authorization by selecting the FULL AUTHORIZATION button after you insert the characteristic.

The other four authorization objects were inserted automatically as soon you selected INSERT SPECIAL CHARACTERISTICS. This approach is essential. If you do not insert the special characteristic, your authorizations will not function downstream. The four characteristics originating from technical content have the following meanings:

- **0TCAACTVT**
  Defines the activity that a user may execute (example: 03 – display).
- **0TCAIPROV**
  Defines the InfoProvider for which the user will be authorized later on. In this case, it's a full authorization that is not limited to one InfoProvider).
- **0TCAKYFNM**
  Controls the authorizations for key figures. You can define the key figures that the user will later be able to use in a report. In this case, it's a full authorization for all key figures.
- **0TCAVALID**
  Defines the validity of the authorization. Here you have an option to define periods for which the authorization is valid. This option is helpful if you review authorizations annually and want to have them automatically expire after a year.

Caution

After the technical migration, the four InfoObjects from the technical content are not yet flagged as relevant to authorization. You still have to set the flag to ensure that the analysis authorizations function correctly. In some cases, you might also have to transfer the four characteristics from the Business Content.

Every analysis authorization must contain the four objects, even if you do not define any limits. In this case, you define the full authorization four times.

You can use details to define the values for which a characteristic should be limited for each row (see Figure 5.6).

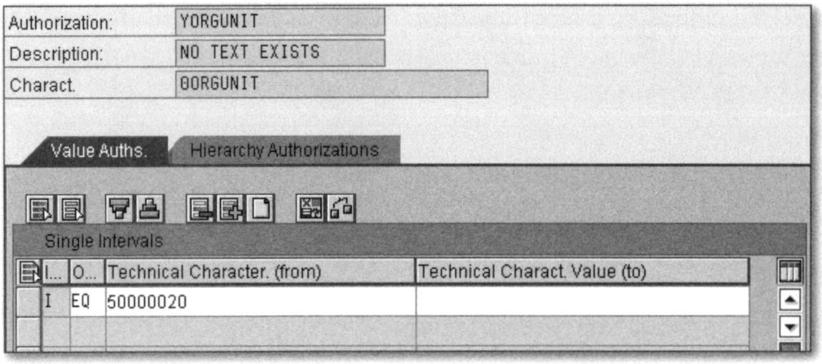

Figure 5.6 Assigning Authorizations in the Detail View

The detail view is split into VALUE AUTHORIZATIONS and HIERARCHY AUTHORIZATIONS. In the VALUE AUTHORIZATIONS tab, you can list individual values or sets of values for which the user should have authorization.

Caution

Note that you can work only with the I (include) option for characteristics and key figures, which means that authorizations such as "All organizational units except 50000020" are impossible. You can resolve this situation by adding the following two rows:

- I, BT, 00000000, 50000019
- I, BT, 50000021, 99999999

The first row includes all organizational units between 00000000 and 50000019 (BT stands for "between"); the second row contains all organizational units above 500000021. This approach excludes organizational unit 50000020.

You can use the HIERARCHY AUTHORIZATIONS tab to define authorizations for hierarchy nodes. First, you define the Hierarchy for which a user should have authorization. Then, you define one or more Nodes, the Type of Authorization, and the Validity Range of the hierarchy (see Figure 5.7).

The hierarchy type defines the areas for which the authorization is to apply. You can select from the following types:

- Authorization only for the selected notes.
- Authorization for the subtree beneath the nodes.
- Authorization for the subtree beneath the nodes, including a level number that you absolutely must create. You maintain the number in the hierarchy level input field.

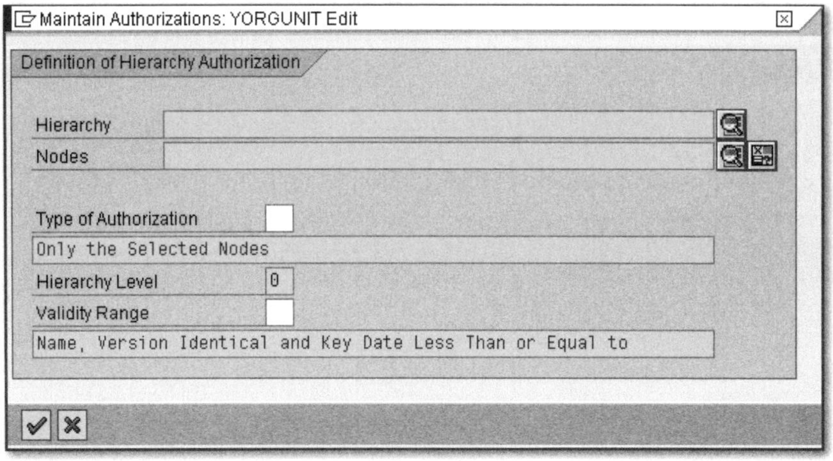

Figure 5.7 Definition of the Hierarchy Authorization

- Authorization for the complete hierarchy.
- Authorization for the subtree beneath the nodes, including a level number for the node that you can create. You maintain the number in the HIERARCHY LEVEL input field.

The validity range indicates how precisely a hierarchy authorization must agree with a selected display hierarchy so that it's subject to an authorization check. The following four values are distinguished:

- Type 0 corresponds to a very strict agreement. The name, version, and validity date must agree, depending on the reporting key date.
- Type 1 checks only the name and version of the hierarchy; the validity does not play a role.
- Type 2 assigns an authorization when the name of the hierarchy is identical; version and validity period do not play a role here.
- Type 3 turns off the authorization check according to the preceding criteria; no more authorization checks are performed.

Take to heart the rule that authorizations should be created as narrowly as possible.

5.1.2 Assigning the Authorization

You can now assign the authorization to users directly, which is a good idea when you work with a relatively small number of users and authorizations. However, you should not take this approach when dealing with several analysis authorizations and users for administrative reasons.

Normally, you assign the analysis authorization of a role using Transaction PFCG (role maintenance), and then the role is assigned to a user or to user groups. The analysis authorization is included with authorization object S_RS_AUTH (see Figure 5.8).

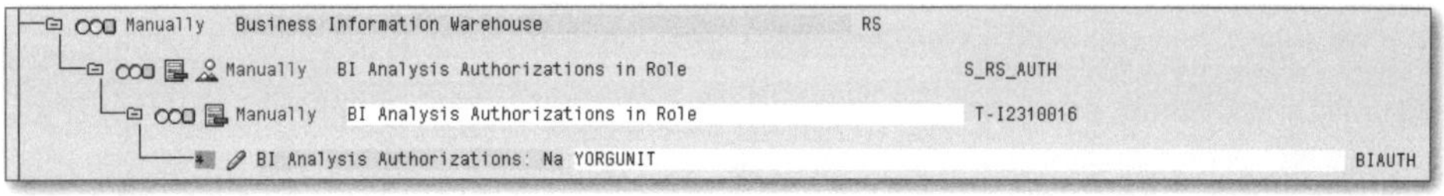

Figure 5.8 Including Analysis Authorization YORGUNIT in a Role with Authorization Object S_RS_AUTH

The following subsection compares the two authorization concepts.

5.1.3 Comparing the Authorization Concepts

The greatest difference between the authorization concepts of SAP BW 3.5 and SAP NetWeaver BI is the technical foundation of the authorization. In the old release, reporting authorizations are based on SAP authorization objects. You had to create specific SAP authorization objects with Transaction RSSM for every InfoObject that you wanted to protect. Authorization in SAP NetWeaver BI, however, is based on the new analysis authorization that no longer has anything in common with SAP authorization objects (except that analysis authorizations must be linked with authorization object S_RS_AUTH when used in roles).

In addition to this technical difference, the use of the reporting authorization from SAP BW 3.5 has been severely limited. Table 5.1 summarizes the differences, which are also used in various SAP presentations.

In terms of the number of objects that could be recorded, reporting authorizations were limited to 10. The limitation is no longer present in SAP NetWeaver BI. The new product also offers you new options to assign authorizations for navigation attributes. And finally, authorizations are no longer assigned for combinations of InfoObjects and InfoCubes; they are now assigned only for InfoObjects.

	Up to SAP BW 3.5	As of SAP NetWeaver BI
Technical basis	SAP authorization object	Analysis authorization
Maintenance	Cannot be changed later on	Can be changed
Number of objects	10 objects	Unlimited
Navigation attribute	Only at the global level	Individually
Hierarchy authorizations	Separate maintenance with 0TCTAUTHH	Corresponds to a value authorization
Relevance to authorization	By InfoObject *and* InfoCube	Only with the InfoObject setting

Table 5.1 List of the Differences Between Reporting and Analysis Authorization

5.2 Principle of Migrating Authorizations

This section covers the migration process from reporting to analysis in more detail, followed by an example that demonstrates the migration of a reporting authorization.

The migration of the authorization concept is carried out with a migration tool that is part of ABAP report RSEC_MIGRATION. The ABAP report supports you during migration of the reporting authorization and executes the migration according to your specifications. Note, however, that the process normally involves some manual follow-up work, as seen in the warning displayed after you call the report (see Figure 5.9). The simpler the design of your authorization concept, the less work you'll have to perform later on.

SAP indicates that about 80% of the migration process can occur automatically. The remaining 20% requires manual post-processing work. In addition, customer exit variables that were created for 0TCTAUTHH are not part of the migration. For such items, manual work is always needed.

Migration of the authorization concept behaves in a manner similar to that of reporting. Existing objects are not overwritten. They are only regenerated based on the old authorizations, and you can then test the regenerated items and assign them to users.

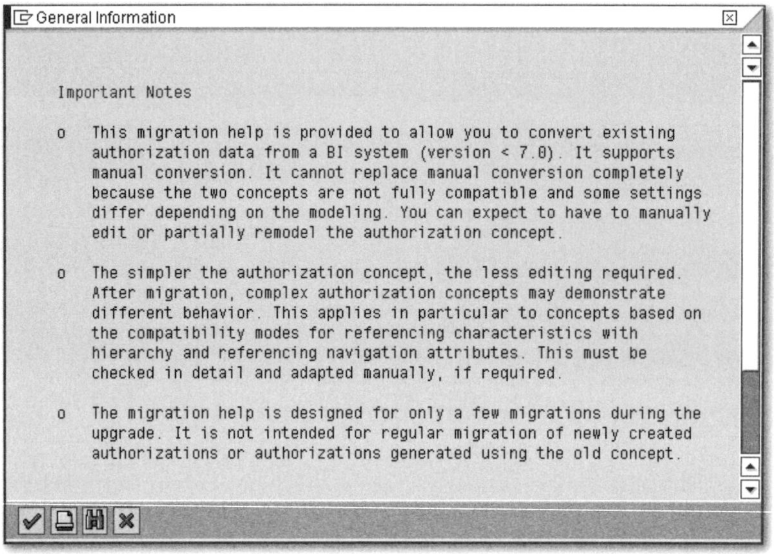

Figure 5.9 Important Notes About Executing Migration Report RSEC_MIGRATION

Report RSEC_MIGRATION begins with a template that you can use to specify the user or users for whom the migration is to be executed (see Figure 5.10).

Note

You can successfully migrate only complete user groups. Accordingly, you should always select the users that belong to a user group. Otherwise, you receive an error message when the report executes: "The migration affects more users than are being migrated." The report then aborts with "return code 8."

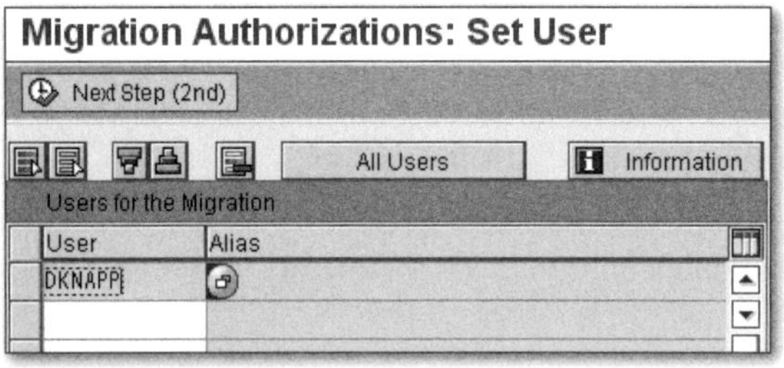

Figure 5.10 Selection of Users for Whom Authorization Will Be Migrated

You then receive a list of the reporting authorization objects that are assigned to a user in an authorization (see Figure 5.11). In the list, you can now define which values of the authorization objects are to be migrated.

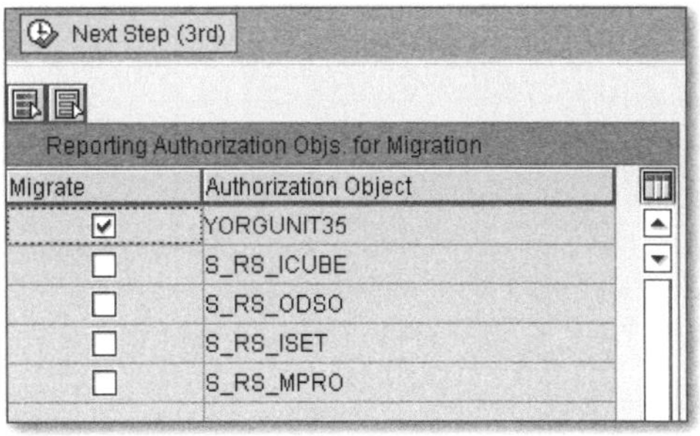

Figure 5.11 Defining the Reporting Authorization Objects That Will Be Migrated

Here, too, note that authorization objects S_RS_ICUBE, S_RS_MPRO, S_RS_ISET, and S_RS_ODSO are no longer used in SAP NetWeaver BI. Instead, you can use InfoObjects 0TCAIPROV, 0TCAACTVT, and 0TCAVALID from the technical content. During migration, they are populated according to the entries in the fields noted previously.

After you've selected the reporting authorization objects, you must define the assignment method (see Figure 5.12). You can select from the following three methods:

- **Direct Assignment to Users**
  With direct assignment, the users selected at the beginning are assigned directly to the new authorizations. No new authorization profiles are created, and no changes are made to roles. After the migration, you can check and change the assignment using Transaction RSU01. In technical terms, this step generates new analysis authorizations that you can then maintain with Transaction RSECADMIN.
- **Generate New Profile**
  This method creates new authorization profiles. For each authorization, you receive a new profile that you can implement in a new role concept. The old role concept remains in place. The technical names of the new profiles begin with RSR_ and an eight-digit number.
- **Enhance Existing Profile**
  This option enhances existing analysis authorizations with authorization object

S_RS_AUTH, in which a new analysis authorization is created for each reporting authorization. The migration tool attempts to maintain the profile with as few changes as possible.

- **Undo Migration**
  Here you have an option to undo an earlier migration completely. Created profiles are deleted. Additional S_RS_AUTH authorization objects that have received new analysis authorizations are kept, but they no longer have any values.

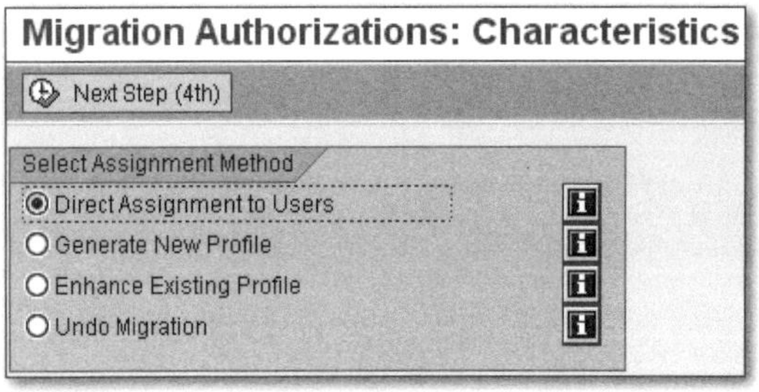

Figure 5.12 Selecting the Migration Method

You select direct assignment when you have a simple authorization concept with a limited scope and only a few users. This option is inappropriate in all other cases.

If you have many roles in which you maintain reporting authorizations, we recommend that you generate new authorization profiles. The old role concept is maintained, and you receive a new role concept that you can assign to users as profiles during migration.

You should enhance existing profiles with some caution because it involves the role concept. Roles are kept in their original condition and enhanced with authorization object S_RS_AUTH. All other authorization profiles remain untouched.

Caution

If you use Transaction PFCG to regenerate an authorization profile, you can remove from the migration any entries that were inserted by the third option.

The execution of the report generates an application log that is displayed after execution. If you close it, you can reopen it using Transaction SLG1 (object RSEC_BW_AUTH, subobject MIGRATE).

The following section shows you this ultimately very simple process with the use of an example.

5.3 Sample Migration

To begin, the authorization is introduced in the old SAP BW 3.5 system and then migrated.

5.3.1 Authorizations in SAP BW

In SAP BW, authorizations are created with Transaction RSSM, in which you can define authorization objects. The SAP BW authorization to be migrated is based on authorization object YORGUNIT35 and consists of InfoObject Organizational Unit (0ORGUNIT), as illustrated in Figure 5.13.

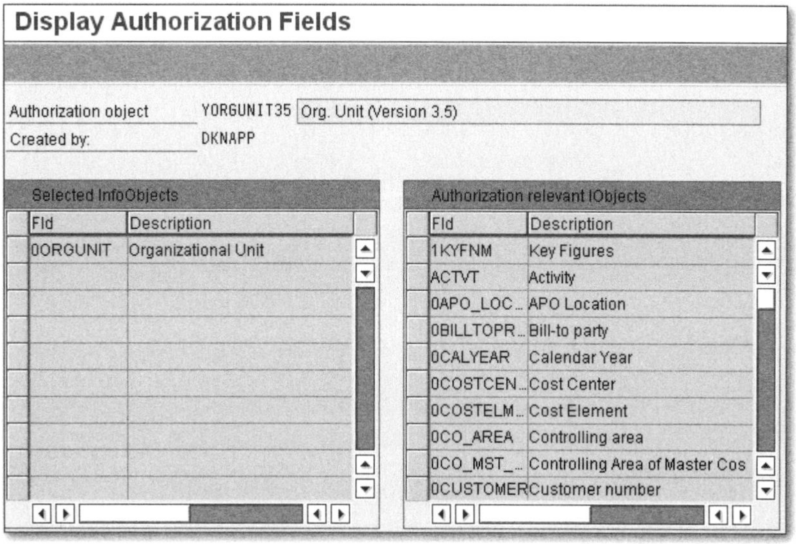

Figure 5.13 SAP BW 3.5 Authorization Object YORGUNIT35 from Transaction RSSM

As you saw in Section 5.1, Authorization Concepts, reporting authorizations in SAP BW can run only with a combination of InfoObject and InfoProvider. Accordingly, after you maintain the authorization objects, you must check the InfoProviders to which the authorization should apply (see Figure 5.14). In this example, we link the authorization with InfoCube Personnel Management (IC_PERMNG).

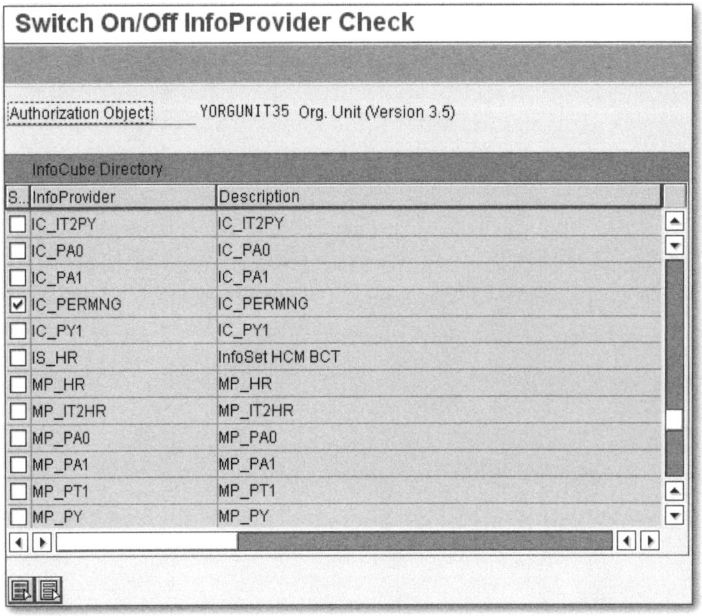

Figure 5.14 Turning on a Check of InfoProvider Personnel Management

You have now generated an SAP authorization object that can be checked against and used on InfoCube Personnel Management and InfoObject Organizational Unit. To define any limitations and to assign the new object to a user, you must define a role in Transaction PFCG. The new authorization object must be present in the role (see Figure 5.15).

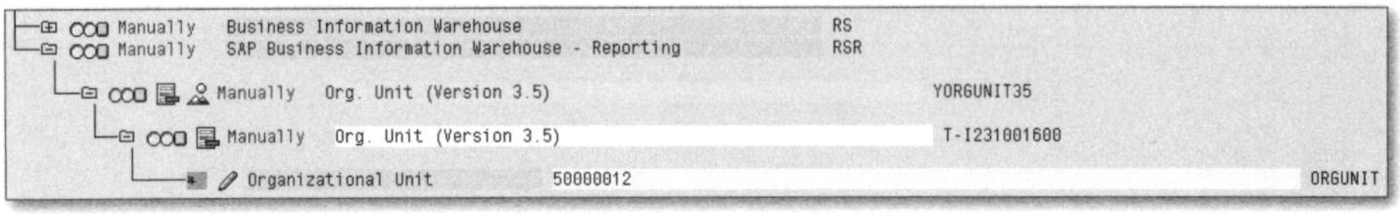

Figure 5.15 Role YORGUNIT35_ROLE with Its Related Authorization Object

The role used here is named YORGUNIT35_ROLE and consists only of SAP BW authorization object YORGUNIT35, which was just created. The authorization was limited so that all users of this group have access to organizational unit 50000012 but not to any other unit.

The authorization was assigned to user BI_DKNAPP, who belongs to user group SAPBW35. The group was created so that we only have to migrate one user.

Note

In addition to role YORGUNIT35_ROLE, user BI_DKNAPP also has a standard role that controls the access to SAP Business Explorer. But because the role is irrelevant to migration, it isn't discussed further here.

5.3.2 Migrating the Authorization

The authorization created in this manner will be automatically migrated with report RSEC_MIGRATION. After confirming the warning message, you must enter one or more users who will be migrated. Here, user BI_DKNAPP is selected.

The report then automatically knows which authorization objects the user has. In this case, reporting authorization YORGUNIT35 is selected and will be migrated (see Figure 5.16).

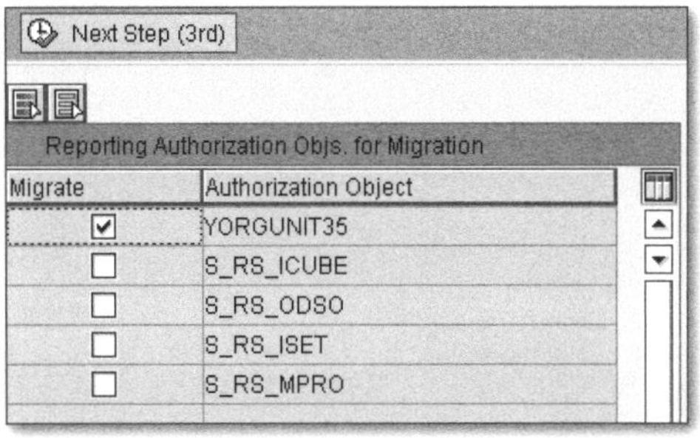

Figure 5.16 Selecting the Authorization to Be Migrated: YORGUNIT35

In the next step, you must define which method the migration will use. You can choose among the following methods:

- Direct Assignment to Users
- Generate New Profile
- Enhance Existing Profile

Because we're dealing with a simple example here, we could select Direct Assignment to Users. In the real world, however, this option is rarely used. We'll select the second option, Generate New Profile, because this first step should not touch the old profiles (see Figure 5.17).

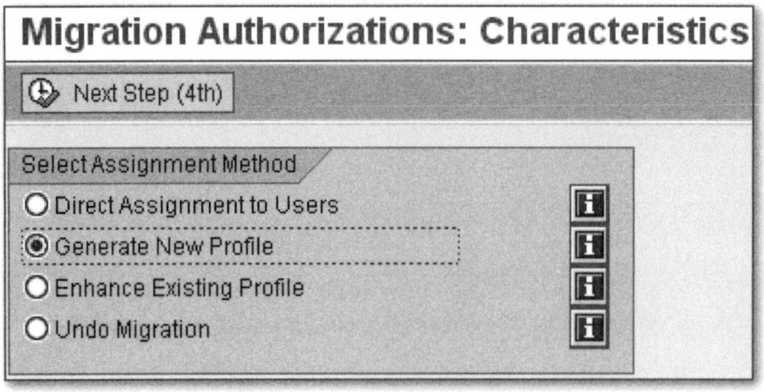

Figure 5.17 Method Selection: Generate New Profile

A screen is then displayed that shows the details of the migration and the characteristics. These options refer to compatibility with earlier versions of SAP BW (before SAP BW 3.0). Here you decide if you also want to generate authorizations and authorization copies for the listed options, which means that you can assign the same authorizations to navigation attributes that you used for the objects defined previously. In this case, you don't define an option because you don't need compatibility with earlier versions (see Figure 5.18).

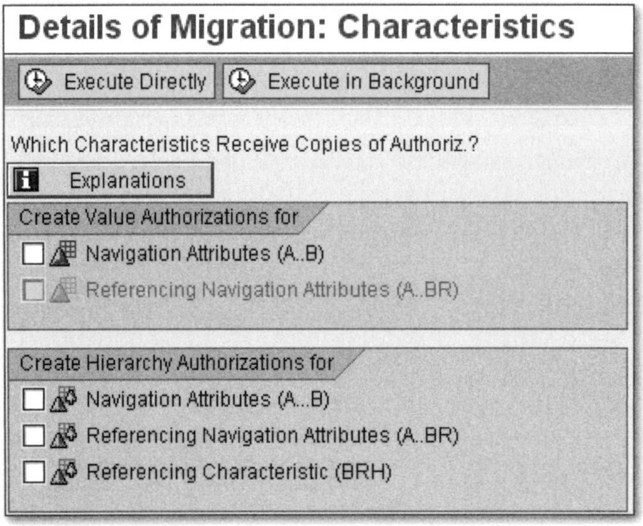

Figure 5.18 Maintaining the Details of the Migration

But maintenance of the last option, Standard Value for Authorization-Relevant Characteristics is pretty important. This option checks the assignment to the InfoProviders created in the old Transaction RSSM. Because authorizationYORGUNIT35 can consist only of a subset of InfoObjects that are relevant to authorizations, they would not be able to run after the migration because all of the InfoObjects that are relevant to authorization must be contained in an analysis authorization. This option now defines the enhancements for the analysis authorization if characteristics are found that were not contained in it. In this case, we click on FULL AUTHORIZATION because the old reporting authorization supported limitations only for the organizational unit. The report can then be executed directly.

You then receive a log that contains information on the errors (if any) that occurred during execution (see Figure 5.19).

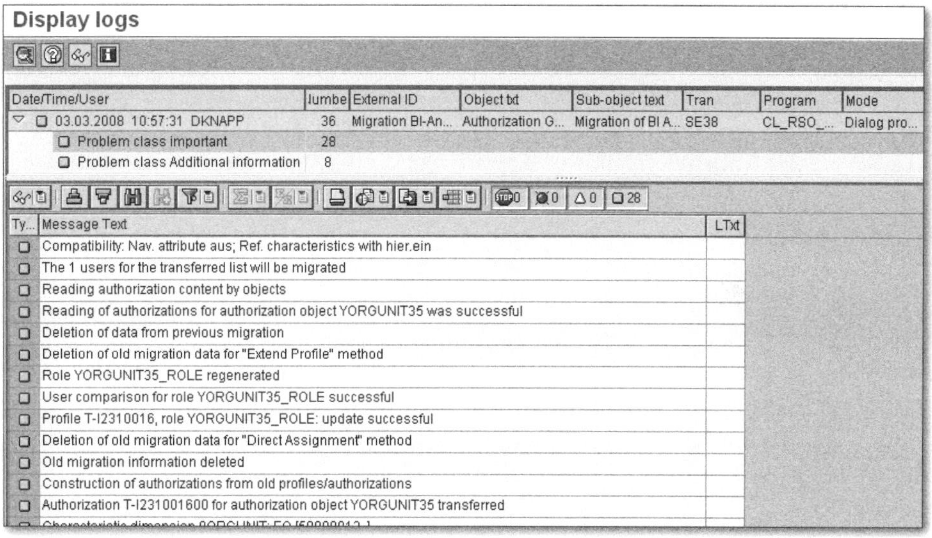

Figure 5.19 Log After Execution of the Migration

As you can see, report RSEC_MIGRATION created a new profile, RSR_00000001, which it assigned to user BI_DKNAPP. The report also generated a new analysis authorization from authorization object YORGUNIT35 and named it YORGUNIT3500.

You can select the new analysis authorization, YORGUNIT3500, in Transaction RSECADMIN. You received an informative text that you could use to recognize it (see Figure 5.20). If you then want to change the authorization later on, you receive a note that you are working with a generated authorization.

BI Authoriz.	Short Descripti...	Medium Descripti...	Long Descripti...
0BI_ALL			
YORGUNIT			
YORGUNIT3500			

Figure 5.20 Selection of the Migrated Authorization

You can now see what the report did with the old reporting authorization (see Figure 5.21).

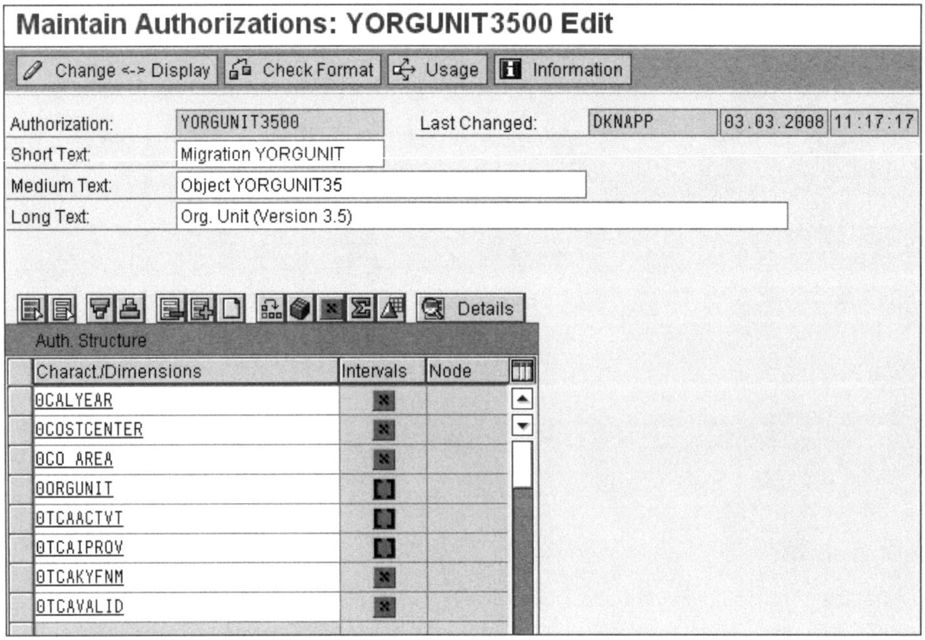

Figure 5.21 Maintenance of Generated AuthorizationYORGUNIT3500

The following activities occurred:

- All of the InfoObjects relevant to authorization contained in InfoProvider IC_PERMNG were added to the full authorization (0CALYEAR, 0COSTCENTER, and 0CO_AREA).

- All standard authorizations that must be contained in every analysis authorization were inserted (0TCAACTVT, 0TCAIPROV, 0TCAKYFNM, and 0TCAVALID).
- The standard authorizations and the limitation from the role for the organizational unit were copied.

Put more precisely, the organization unit contains a limitation for value 50000012, the activity for value 03 (display), and the InfoProvider for value IC_PERMNG. The migration was successful, and you can now remove the old authorization profiles.

5.3.3 Other Assignment Methods

If you select an assignment method different from the one selected in step 3, role YORGUNIT35_ROLE is inserted and enhanced with the new profile. In Transaction PFCG in maintenance of the authorization, you can see that a new authorization based on authorization object S_RS_AUTH was added (see Figure 5.22) and linked to the generated analysis authorization, YORGUNIT3500. The old branch of the authorization was not touched.

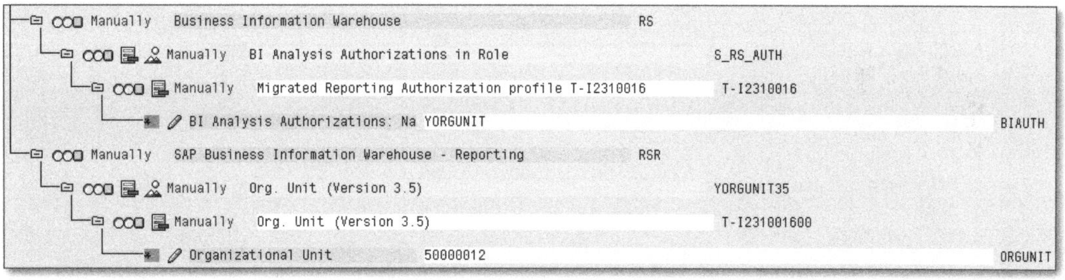

Figure 5.22 An Edited Role from the Migration Report After the Migration

When you select this method, you can set the old authorization branch to inactive after a successful test.

Reporting authorizations are, by design, controlled with variables that are created with authorization variables. After the migration, the variables are always still present and don't need to be adjusted because they have a standard replacement path for authorizations. No extra work is required here.

5.4 Recommendations for a Migration Project

In the previous section, you learned how you can use the migration report to transfer authorizations from SAP BW and how the report functions. In any case, the migration report migrates only simple concepts smoothly and still requires manual follow-up work.

The 80/20 ratio of automatic to manual migration noted earlier is basically correct. Nevertheless, these numbers can vary, so that the 20% of manual work actually takes up far more than 20% of the time that an automatic migration requires. In addition, these numbers don't include the test phase that must be performed thoroughly because of the sensitivity of the data.

The report always reaches its limits when too many users with various authorizations are processed simultaneously. You can resolve this problem by creating temporary user groups on the development system with Transaction SUGR to migrate only subsets of the actual users who must be migrated. That approach lowers the complexity of authorization objects (see Figure 5.23). This approach was used in Section 5.3.2 to reduce the number of users.

Figure 5.23 Maintenance of User Groups with Transaction SUGR

In this phase, schedule enough time for the migration. The report itself runs for only a few minutes, but testing the generated authorization and the correct functioning of the objects that are involved along with the reporting authorizations consumes a great deal of time.

5.5 Summary

In this chapter, you learned about how the new analysis authorization functions and how it differs from the old concept of SAP authorization objects by providing more options when assigning authorizations and requiring manual adjustments when you migrate authorizations.

You then learned about Report RSEC_MIGRATION for migrating authorizations from SAP BW into the new analysis authorization of SAP NetWeaver BI. Specifically, we covered the following steps of the report:

1. Defining users
2. Selecting the authorization objects to be migrated
3. Selecting the assignment method
4. Maintaining the details of the migration

After executing the report, you generated new authorization profiles and, if you selected the appropriate assignment method, roles that have been adjusted according to their old authorizations. You saw an example that demonstrated how the report works.

The chapter concluded with an examination of the critical factors and time that a migration can require.

6 Migration in Reporting

In this chapter, the term "reporting" refers to all reporting functions in the SAP data warehouse. Due to the technological evolution of SAP BW 3.5 into SAP NetWeaver BI, reporting is currently the cost driver of concept migration.

To explain exactly why a time-consuming migration of reporting is necessary, this chapter opens by examining the similar yet technologically diverse designs of both versions. The designs are examined in detail to facilitate a discussion of the necessary migration. Next, we'll turn to the general principle of how reporting can be migrated, which is illustrated here with detailed examples. As in previous chapters, this chapter closes with a discussion of cost considerations and some real-world applications.

6.1 Functional Design in Reporting

Reporting is based on the same functional design in both SAP BW 3.5 and SAP NetWeaver BI but is implemented using different technology in each case. We'll therefore begin by examining the functional design, before turning our attention to the technological differences.

6.1.1 The Query as a Fundamental Concept

Datasets in a data warehouse are usually stored in one-dimensional format. Special techniques are required to access a multidimensional dataset. In SAP BW and SAP NetWeaver BI, the technique used is a query, which can be implemented using a graphical application and represents the starting point for multidimensional querying of the dataset. Queries are created with the BEx Query Designer from the SAP Business Explorer Suite (BEx). This brings us full circle in terms of definitions because queries provide a starting point for the definition of InfoProviders.

InfoProviders

InfoProviders are BI objects for which a query can be created. InfoProviders may physically contain data (InfoCubes, DataStore objects, InfoObjects) or represent virtual views of data (VirtualProviders, MultiProviders, InfoSets).

To display a report in any format requires a query. After you create a query, you then have additional options for designing the layout or selecting the display format (see Figure 6.1).

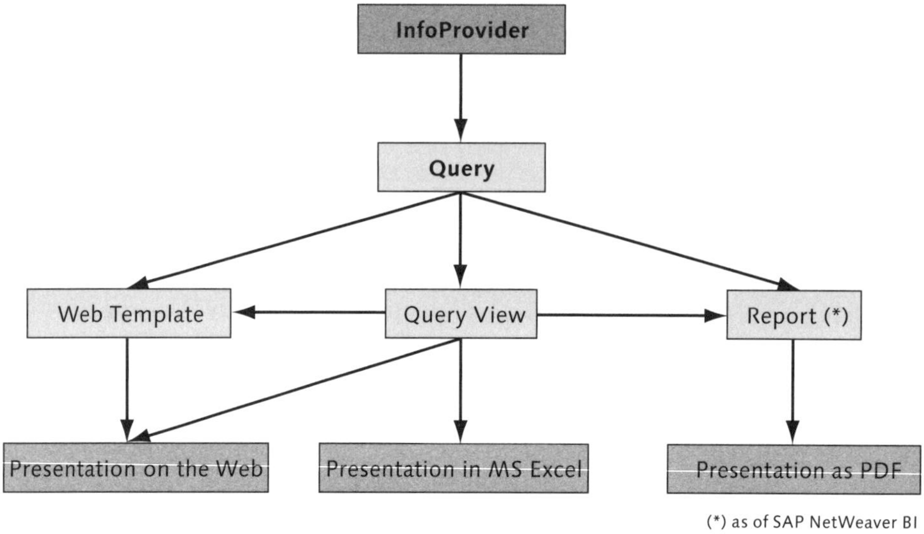

Figure 6.1 Display Formats and Options in Reporting

Queries can be displayed directly on the Web if you use a standard web template provided by SAP. You can use a *web template* (or *web application*) to display the query in graphical format on the Web. Alternatively, you can use the BEx Web Application Designer (WAD) from the SAP Business Explorer Suite to design your own web templates, which you can then display on the Web.

SAP Standard Web Template

The SAP standard web template was created by SAP using the Web Application Designer and defined in Customizing. It allows you to display queries in a predefined format.

In SAP BW 3.5, the technical name of the standard web template was 0ANALYZER, and the corresponding name in SAP NetWeaver BI is 0ANALYSIS_PATTERN. In SAP NetWeaver BI, the SAP standard web template is often also referred to as BEx Web Analyzer.

In addition to web display, you can also access queries directly in Microsoft Excel or export them from the Web to Excel.

A *query view* (or *view* for short) is a saved view of the query data. It allows you to save filter settings and navigation steps and use these again the next time you call the view. For example, key figures are often sorted in ascending or descending order. You can create a view in the Web Analyzer or in Microsoft Excel in the BEx Analyzer. The standard web template provides elements such as the Save view button for this purpose.

One new feature of SAP NetWeaver BI is the BEx Report Designer, which allows you to output the view as a PDF. To do this, you create a *report* for a specific output format (e.g., DIN A4). This is useful because the scrolling option can't be transferred from the Web onto paper. Reports cannot be migrated because the Report Designer did not exist in SAP BW 3.5.

Support for the BEx Report Designer

After its purchase of the French company Business Objects, SAP announced that development of the BEx Report Designer would not continue beyond 2008. The last version of the BEx Report Designer will appear in SAP NetWeaver 7.1 at the end of 2008. As of 2009, the Xcelsius solution from Business Objects will be replaced by Xcelsius+. However, maintenance support for the Report Designer will continue until 2016. For more information, refer to the SAP Developer Network (*https://sdn.sap.com*) under Business Objects.

Table 6.1 lists the reporting objects and their applications.

The query, query view, and web template reporting objects are available in both SAP BW 3.5 and SAP NetWeaver BI. However, reports can only be created with SAP NetWeaver BI. These are based on 3.5 queries, 3.5 queries that have already been migrated, or queries newly created with SAP NetWeaver BI.

Reporting Object	Application from the SAP Business Explorer Suite
Query	BEx Query Designer
Query view	BEx Analyzer or BEx Web Analyzer
Web template	BEx Web Application Designer
Report	BEx Report Designer

Table 6.1 Table 6.1 Reporting Objects and Their Applications

Naming Conventions

To distinguish clearly between new and old queries, queries from SAP BW 3.5 are referred to here as 3.5 queries, whereas queries from SAP NetWeaver BI are referred to as 7.0 queries. The same approach is applied to web templates.

The following subsection provides a brief introduction to the applications used to create queries and web templates and the differences between these applications in the two SAP releases.

6.1.2 BEx Query Designer

You use the BEx Query Designer (see Figure 6.2) to create a query for a multidimensional dataset. The Query Designer defines the objects that can be evaluated when you execute the query.

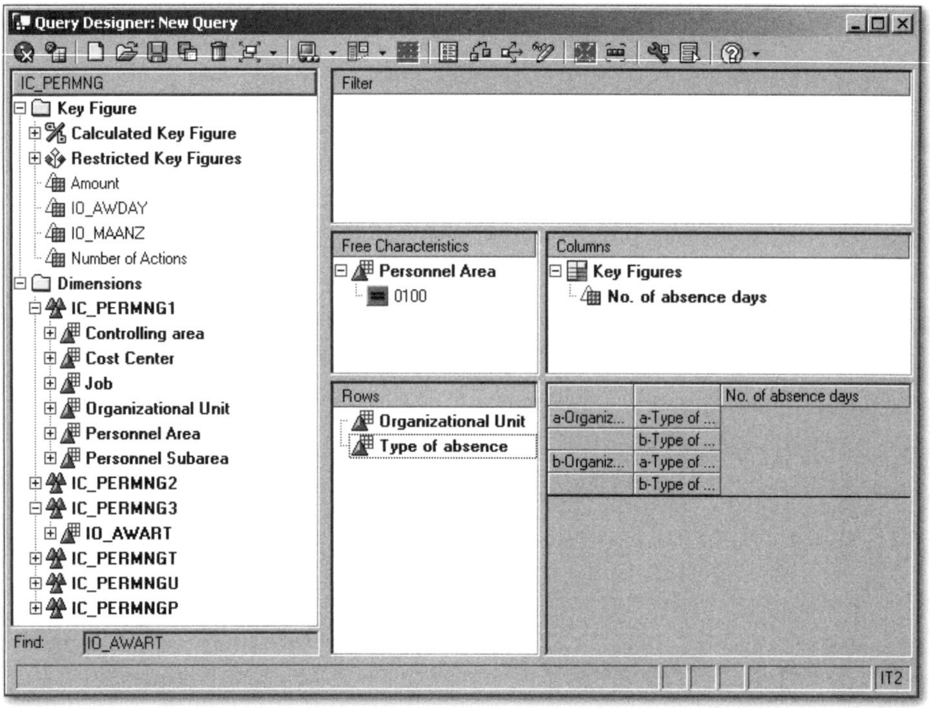

Figure 6.2 BEx Query Designer in SAP BW 3.5

As stated at the start of the chapter, a query is always based on an InfoProvider, which is displayed here on the left, together with all of its characteristics and key figures. These can then be used for evaluation in the rows and columns. In this example, the report consists of a list of all types of absences and the absence days per organizational unit for Personnel Area 0100. The preview in the bottom-right corner gives you an idea of how the report will appear later.

The FREE CHARACTERISTICS area contains objects that can be used for navigation or for filtering on the Web or in Excel after the report is executed. If you place the PERSONNEL subarea in the FREE CHARACTERISTICS area, for example, you can add additional filters or breakdowns by personnel area after you execute the report.

In the FILTER area at the top, you can define characteristic restrictions, which are invisible in the report and cannot be changed. If, for example, you want to define a restriction for a specific organizational unit that you don't want the user to see, you can do this in the FILTER area.

Figure 6.3 shows the same query from the preceding example in the BEx Query Designer in SAP NetWeaver BI 7.0.

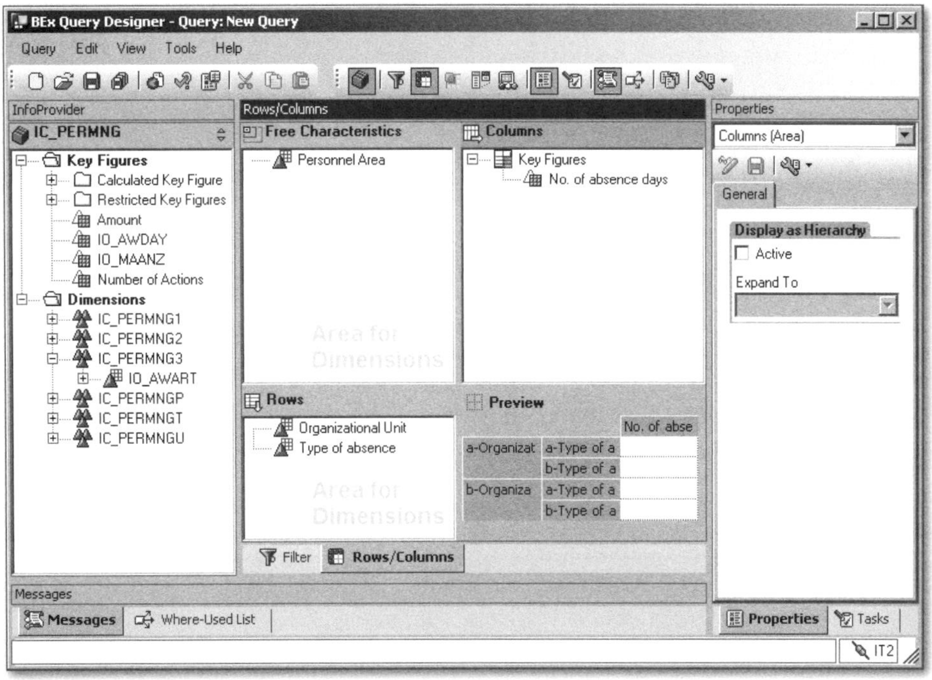

Figure 6.3 BEx Query Designer in SAP NetWeaver BI

The underlying principle of the Query Designer in terms of the positioning of rows and columns remains unchanged. However, the original ROWS, COLUMNS, PREVIEW, FREE CHARACTERISTICS, and FILTER areas are now divided between the following two tabs:

- **Filter tab**
  The FILTER tab contains default values and characteristic restrictions. The characteristic restrictions are identical to the FILTER area in Query Designer 3.5. However, the default values represent a modified view of the FREE CHARACTERISTICS. Although you could restrict characteristics directly in the ROWS, COLUMNS, and FREE CHARACTERISTICS areas with Query Designer 3.5, you must define these restrictions in the DEFAULT VALUES area in Query Designer 7.0. This is why it appears at first glance in Figure 6.3 as though no restriction has been made for the PERSONNEL area. The restriction is in fact hidden on the other tab.
- **Rows/Columns tab**
  The ROWS/COLUMNS tab still contains the familiar view comprising ROWS, COLUMNS, FREE CHARACTERISTICS, and the PREVIEW.

Additional Tabs

If you use advanced techniques, such as Conditions and Exceptions, two additional tabs of the same name are also shown. These are discussed in Section 6.3, Sample Migration of a Query.

The PROPERTIES area on the extreme right is another new feature of the new Query Designer. In the older version, you could only access these settings through the function menu. Both versions are examined in greater detail in Section 6.3, Sample Migration of a Query.

Performance of the BEx Query Designer

The Business Explorer Suite is a collection of applications that you can install on your client PC. Performance, which was good in SAP BW 3.5, has significantly declined with SAP NetWeaver BI because the applications were newly developed, and not only the SAP NetWeaver BI server but also the SAP NetWeaver Portal is required to respond to requests.

6.1.3 BEx Web Application Designer

The Web Application Designer allows you to develop your own web templates, which can be used for a specific query or as a default web template. A web template is always based on at least one query, which is then displayed, for example in a diagram. Figure 6.4 shows the Web Application Designer from SAP BW 3.5.

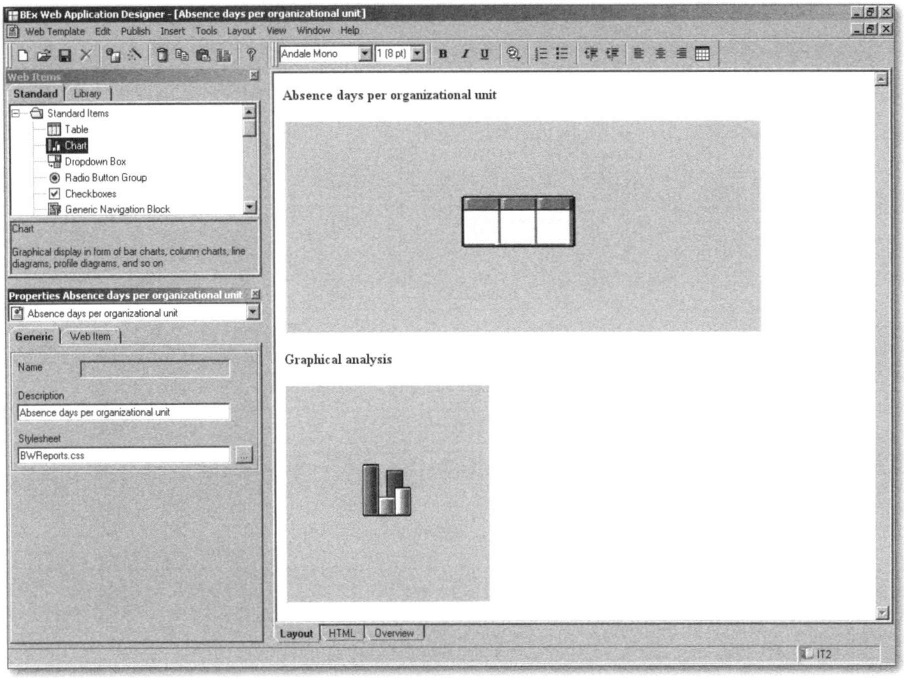

Figure 6.4 BEx Web Application Designer in SAP BW 3.5

The Web Application Designer is divided into the following three areas:

- **Web Items area**
  On the top left, you will see predefined graphical objects, which you can use to display queries (e.g., tables, charts, drop-down boxes etc.).
- **Properties area**
  Below the graphical objects area, the Properties area is where you can maintain the properties of web templates and all of the web items they contain.
- **Layout area**
  In this largest area, you can position elements from the Web Items area. You can edit these graphically in the layout view or by using the HTML source code

in the HTML view. Although the layout view offers limited flexibility, you can "pull out all the stops" in the HTML view and use everything from HTML to CSS or JavaScript to design your layout.

The objects that you place in the layout view are indicated by a red `<object>` tag in the HTML view so that you can find them again easily. In addition to these `<object>` tags, a range of internal SAP BW macros (referred to as *commands*) are similarly highlighted in red after they are used. These macros are used to change filter settings, call different URLs, or read language-dependent text from ABAP programs, for example. They are discussed in detail in Section 6.4, Sample Migration of a Web Template.

The structure of the Web Application Designer remains essentially the same. Figure 6.5 shows the new version with the same web template.

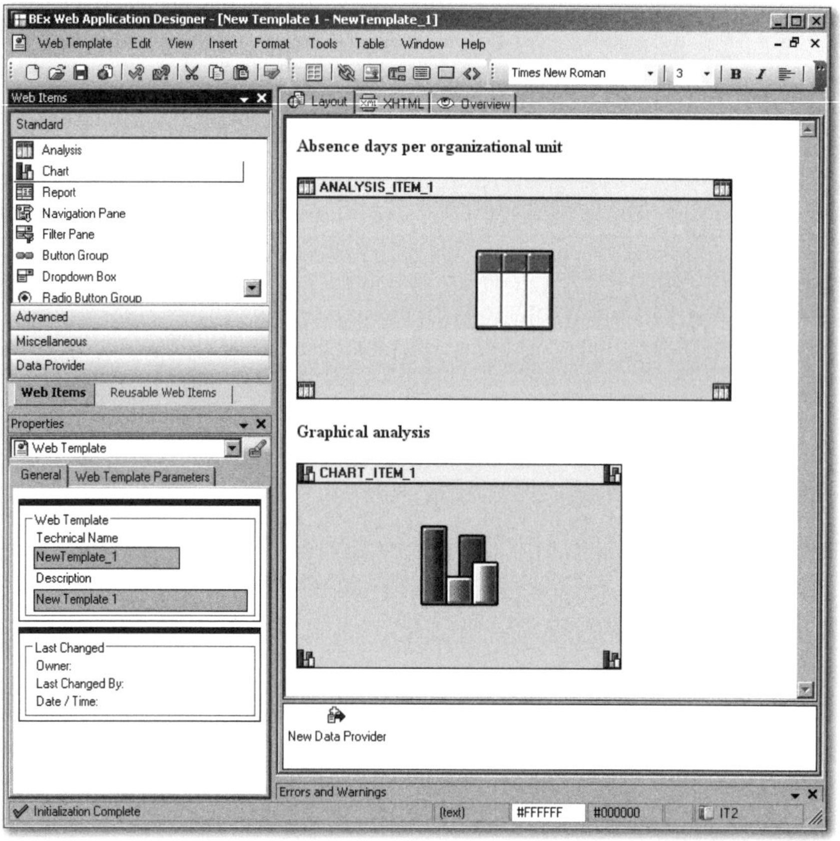

Figure 6.5 BEx Web Application Designer in SAP NetWeaver BI

The new Web Application Designer is divided into the following three areas: WEB ITEMS, PROPERTIES, and LAYOUT. What is new here is the subdivision of the WEB ITEMS into STANDARD ITEMS and ADVANCED ITEMS, as well as the new names assigned to many of the web items. The old terms and their translations into the new terms are provided in Appendix D, Translation of Web Items, to help you find your way around after the migration if you have been using the old Web Application Designer.

In addition, HTML has been replaced by Extensible Hypertext Markup Language (XHTML). XHTML is an XML-compatible form of HTML, which follows stricter syntax rules.

Example

In HTML, the `<br>` tag is often used for a line break. In XHTML, an opening tag cannot be used without a closing tag, which means that line breaks must be represented by the `<br/>` tag.

As you know, it may be difficult to switch web applications if you use your own source code. This is because the use of JavaScript has also been modified. Furthermore, the discontinuation of certain functions, such as the table interface, makes parts of the migration much more difficult. This problem is dealt with in detail in Section 6.5, Special Considerations When Performing a Migration.

The next section explains the principle of migration in reporting and discusses important points you should be aware of.

6.2 The Principle of Migration in Reporting

As with the migration of the data flow, migration in reporting is not a compulsory process. You only need to perform a migration if you want to use new functions. You can also start the migration with a single report and only continue with further reports after successful testing of the result. You do not necessarily have to migrate all reports.

To allow you to open and edit both old and new SAP NetWeaver BI objects, such as queries and web templates, SAP provides both the old and new version of SAP Business Explorer tools in the new release. The Business Explorer start menu therefore appears as shown in Figure 6.6. This ensures that you can continue to use all reporting tools as normal after the technical migration.

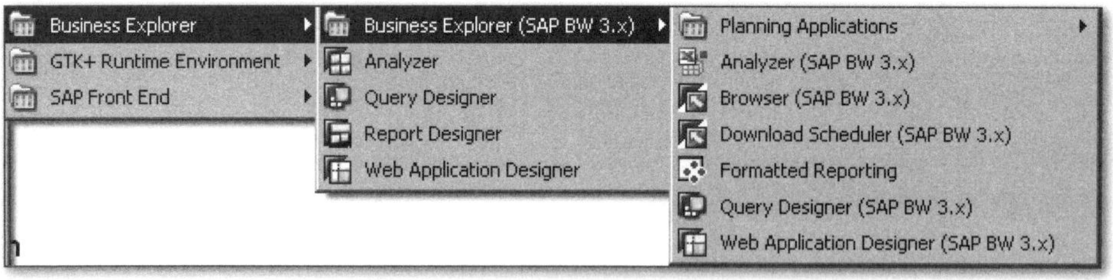

Figure 6.6 Business Explorer Start Menu with Old and New Tools

Prerequisites for Using the Business Explorer

SAP NetWeaver BI requires SAP GUI 6.40 Compilation 5 or higher to run the new Business Explorer tools. These can only be installed if the .NET Framework 1.1 is installed. For more details of the prerequisites, see the end of Section 2.2, Migrating the System Landscape, in Chapter 2.

6.2.1 Migrating Queries

The migration of queries is virtually automatic. Each query is automatically migrated as soon as it's opened and saved in BEx Query Designer 7.0. The old query is overwritten with the new version and can no longer be opened with BEx Query Designer 3.5. To avoid this, save the query under a new technical name. In this respect, the query is an exception object because all other objects in the three areas of data flow, web reporting, and authorizations essentially remain in the old version.

However, the new BEx Report Designer 7.0 and BEx Web Application Designer tools can work with old queries. Therefore, you shouldn't migrate queries in the first step. You should only perform a migration if you want to use the new functions in the Query Designer, for example, new functions for creating exceptions and conditions.

From the point of view of the query, the question of whether the data flow had already been migrated is irrelevant. You can also create a 7.0 query in an InfoProvider with an old data flow. It's equally possible to create a 3.5 query in an

InfoProvider with a migrated data flow. A migration is only required to use new functions.

6.2.2 Migrating Query Views

If you already use query views in web applications, you can continue to use these as normal. Unlike queries, query views are also downward compatible with the old application. If you call and save a query view in a new web application, the query view is saved *in addition to* the old version. This ensures that it can still be used with older web applications. The SAP BW 3.5 format of the query view is not overwritten.

This produces the following behavior:

- The new query view is used in the new web applications.
- The old query view is still used in the old web applications.
- The old query is used when you call the query view with BEx Analyzer.

6.2.3 Migrating Web Templates

The migration of web templates is the most time-consuming part of the migration in reporting. The migration is triggered when you open a 3.5 web template with the migration tool from the new BEx Web Application Designer 7.0. In contrast to the migration of queries or query views, the migration in this case is only partly automatic, in that the old objects from the 3.5 version are transferred to the new version. Due to customer-specific modifications in the form of JavaScript or the use of table interfaces, the remainder of the migration must be performed manually.

The migration produces two independent objects of the same web template in the database, that is, one 3.5 version and one 7.0 version. The two objects are independent of each other, which means that changes to the 3.5 object have no effect on the 7.0 version.

You can continue to use queries and query views in 3.5 format in 7.0 web templates.

The migration of a web template involves the following steps:

1. The migration starts when you open a web template in version 3.5 in the migration tool from Web Application Designer 7.0.

2. After you open the template, the web template is converted into an XHTML-compatible format. This can be done manually or automatically as required.
3. After the migration into an XHTML-compatible format, a dialog box appears, prompting you to finish the migration. Your web template is then displayed in the XHTML view of the Web Application Designer. Any relevant error or warning messages are displayed in the status window.
4. You can still view all of the old SAP BW macros that you've used. You should then convert these into the new format, for example, using the Command Wizard.

When you save the web template, you can give it a new name or keep the old technical name. Note that the old 3.5 version is not overwritten.

6.2.4 Special Considerations When Migrating Web Templates

The migration of web templates is subject to a range of special considerations, which make the job of migration more difficult. You'll find a complete list of these special considerations in SAP Note 832713 ("Migration of web templates from BW 3.x to NetWeaver 2004s"), which is updated on an ongoing basis. Following is a list of the key points (refer to the SAP Note for the full list):

- The BROADCASTER and BROADCASTER INDEX Web items are located in the SAP NetWeaver Portal in SAP NetWeaver BI and therefore can no longer be used in a web template. As a result, these web items are no longer available. The same applies to the ROLE MENU, ABC ANALYSIS, and ALERT MONITOR web items, which are now similarly located in the portal runtime environment.
- As mentioned earlier, many web items have been renamed, and some have been added or removed. Appendix D provides a complete list of objects that have been changed or deleted.
- Many SAP BW macros (or commands as they are also known) have changed in terms of syntax and semantics. Additional manual modifications are required because only some macros can be migrated automatically.
- Most JavaScript functions have become superfluous due to the various types of command definition. Where possible, an attempt is made to map commands to the new command structure during the migration. However, this mapping is not complete.

- The table interface or Web Design API for tables is no longer available. No replacement for this function is currently planned. However, if this function is re-implemented, it won't be automatically possible to migrate it, according to SAP.
- JavaScript statements can only be migrated and used as of Support Package Stack 7 (SPS 7). The use of JavaScript in web templates is not permitted or possible prior to SPS 7, so don't use a system lower than SPS 7. SAP also recommends that you don't use SPS 11–13 in a production environment. Therefore, use SPS 10 or SPS 14 or higher (see Section 2.2, Migrating Individual Systems, in Chapter 2).

The following sections explain how to migrate a query and a web template. This is followed by a discussion of the special considerations that apply to the migration of web templates. This chapter closes with some practical recommendations and a step-by-step guide to performing a migration in this area.

6.3 Sample Migration of a Query

This section provides a sample 3.5 query and 3.5 web template to illustrate migration in reporting. First, let's discuss the query and web template in detail, before turning to the question of how to migrate the query. As you saw in the previous chapter, this process is virtually automatic.

6.3.1 Application Description

The report lists the "Top 10" customers in a calendar year. The calendar year can be filtered in the web template created later. The city in which each company has its headquarters is also shown (see Figure 6.7). The technical name of the query is ZJWRS_T10_2004.

In addition to listing the customers, we want the query to show a ranking (from 1 to 10) before each customer name. Finally, the sales for each customer are to be shown and highlighted in color. Because we want the ranking to be displayed in the first column and the sales figure in the last, the usual rows/columns layout can't be used in this case. The Query Designer allows us to use a table layout instead.

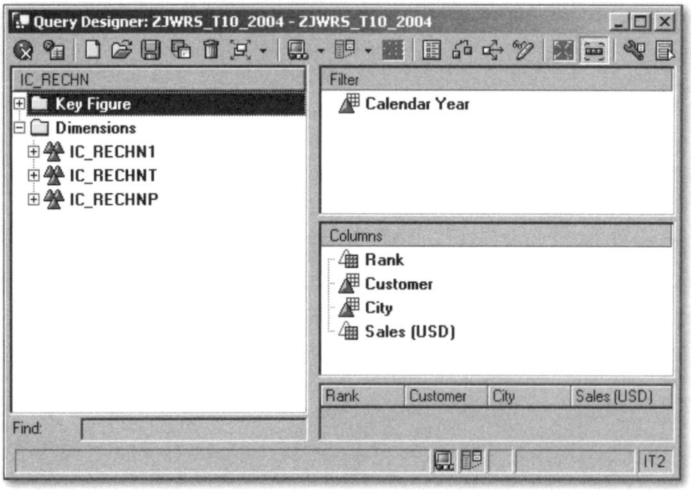

Figure 6.7 Example of a Query for Evaluating a Company's Top 10 Customers

The Top 10 customers are calculated using a condition. You specify that only the top 10 sales figures are to be output (see Figure 6.8).

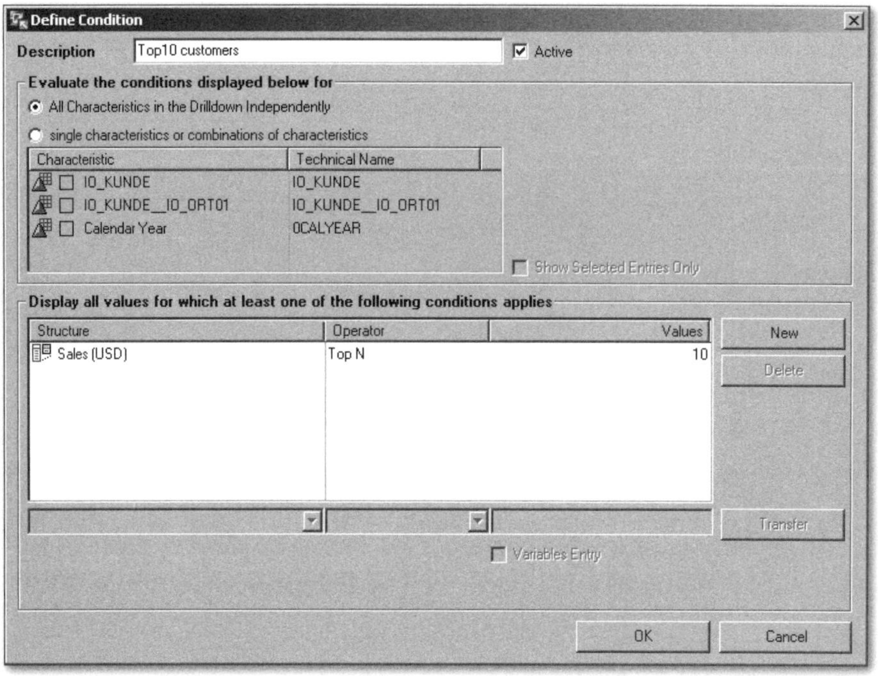

Figure 6.8 Definition of the "Top 10" Condition for Sales Figures

You use *exceptions* to produce color highlighting in the results. You can use an exception to assign various levels to the value ranges of a key figure, which will be highlighted in the results. The definition of exceptions is shown in Figure 6.9.

Exceptions

Exceptions actually indicate particularly critical values, for example, contracts that exceed capacity.

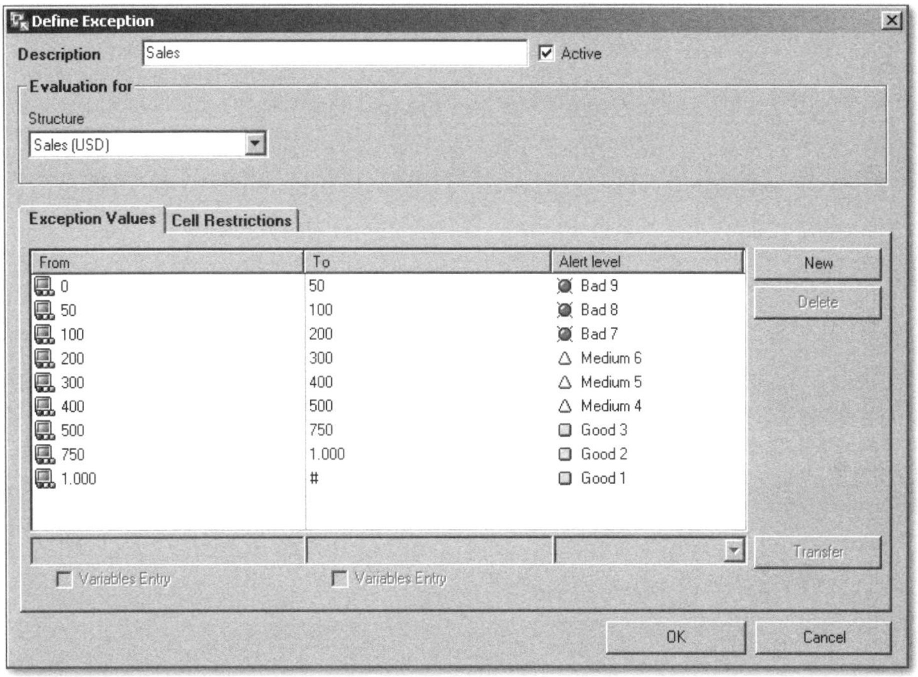

Figure 6.9 Defining Exceptions for Color Highlighting of Sales Figures

Finally, totals rows are only shown for customers. The totals rows for the cities are suppressed. Figure 6.10 shows the final result as it appears on the web.

After the query is executed, a warning message appears in the header of the web template to draw attention to the suppression of the totals rows for cities. This occurs because this suppression may be incompatible with the condition in some cases. In this case, however, the message is irrelevant and is suppressed in the later web template.

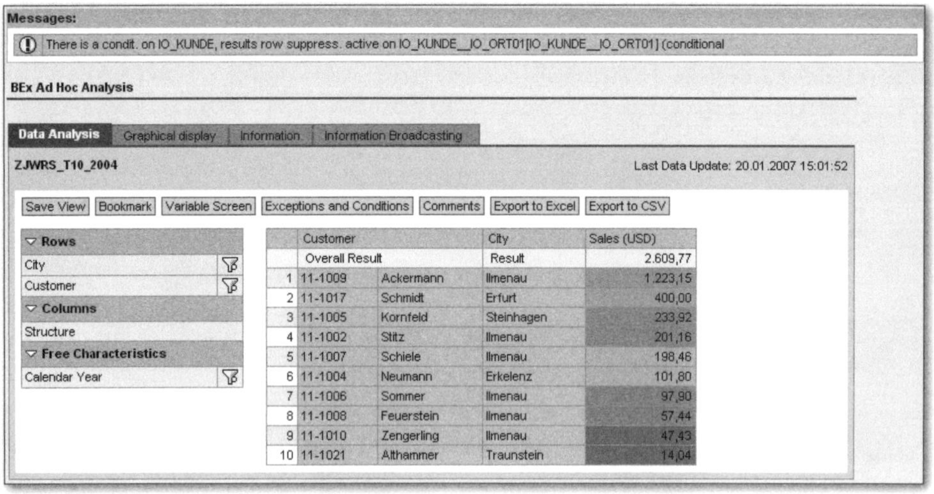

Figure 6.10 Result of the Query on the Web

6.3.2 Migrating the Query

To migrate the query, first open it in the new BEx Query Designer 7.0. It also appears in the history of the most recently edited queries. When you open the query, an error message appears in the status window to draw attention to incorrect exceptions (see Figure 6.11).

Note also that there are a number of differences between the appearance of the query here and how it was created in the old Query Designer. As you can see, the Rank is now shown in the Columns, even though a different layout was selected, namely, the table layout.

This example is intended to illustrate that manual adjustments are possible, despite the information provided by SAP. The first problem is that the tabular view configured in the old Query Designer has disappeared. This is referred to in the Release Notes for Support Package Stack 11:

The mode "Tabular View" was removed from the Query Designer. The BEx Report Designer offers instead numerous options for creating formatted reports. (Source: Release Notes for SAP NetWeaver 7.0 SPS 11, Enterprise Reporting, Query and Analysis).

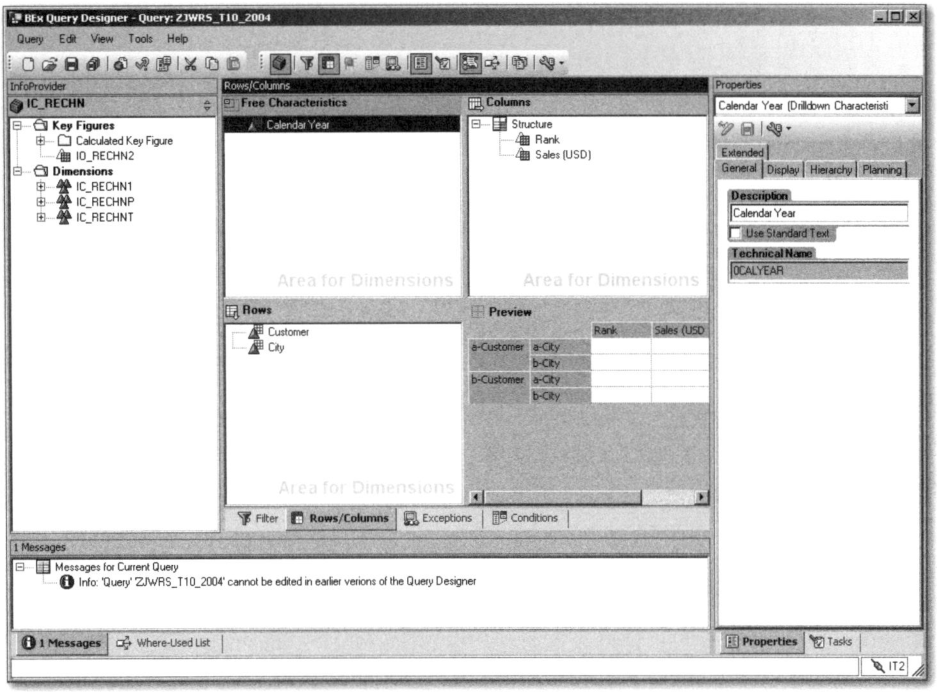

Figure 6.11 Opening a 3.5 Query in the New BEx Query Designer

This means that our only options are to use the rows/columns layout or the BEx Report Designer.

The second problem occurs when we use exceptions. As of SAP NetWeaver BI, these are subject to strict syntax checks, which means that open value ranges, such as [1,000; #], are no longer permitted. This display must be replaced with a zoom command (see Figure 6.12), which is available in the new Query Designer.

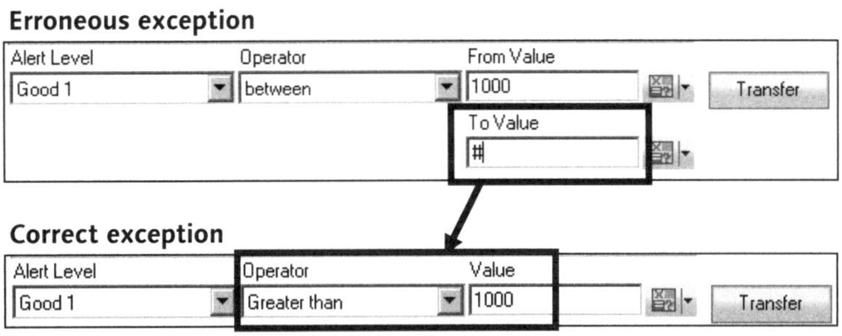

Figure 6.12 Extended Syntax Check and Correction for Exceptions

After you correct the exception, a new warning appears in the message window to notify you that the query can no longer be edited with older versions of the Query Designer. If you then save the query under the same name, a similar message appears when you open the query in the old Query Designer (see Figure 6.13).

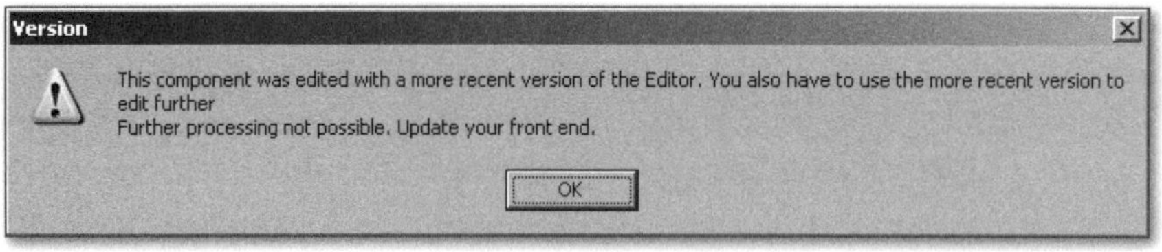

Figure 6.13 Message Displayed When You Open a 7.0 Query in the Old BEx Query Designer

To demonstrate that 7.0 web templates also work with 3.5 queries, we'll save the changed query under a different technical name (ZJWRS_T10_BEX70).

6.3.3 Conclusion

You've seen how you can perform a migration by merely saving a query. However, minor changes may occur, for example, if you used a tabular view or exceptions with open value ranges. On the other hand, the migration is completed within a short space of time.

The next section discusses the appearance of the corresponding web template and how it can be migrated.

6.4 Sample Migration of a Web Template

The migration of web templates is by far the most time-consuming part of the migration process. The process starts automatically but is interrupted by required manual action and almost always results in manual post-processing, depending on how much of your own JavaScript or HTML source code you have used.

The next section follows the structure of the last section and begins by describing the structure of the existing 3.5 web templates before discussing how these are migrated.

6.4.1 Description of the 3.5 Web Template

The web template is based on the 3.5 query with the technical name ZJWRS_T10_2004, which was described in the last section. The technical name of the 3.5 web template is ZJWRS_T10. Figure 6.14 provides an overview of the web template.

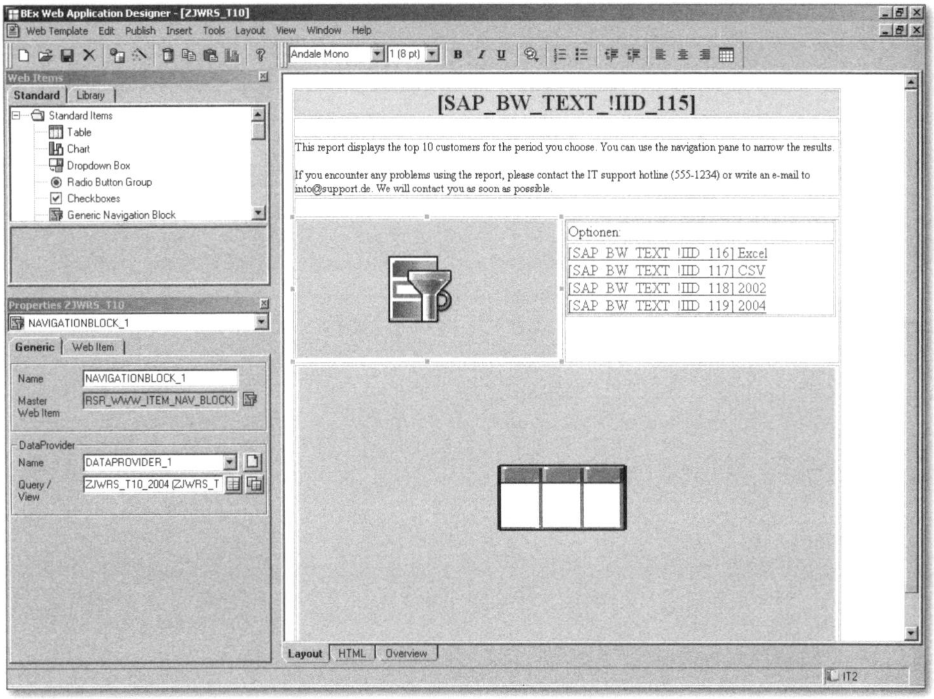

Figure 6.14 Web Template for Migration to SAP NetWeaver BI

The web template includes a centered header, which is currently [SAP_BW_TEXT_!IID_47]. This display, which only appears as shown in the layout view, indicates that the text to be displayed is determined using an ABAP program in the backend, rather than in the web template.

A short description of what the web template does is provided below the header. This text was entered in the web template directly.

Below this description are two table columns. The generic navigation block web item, which you can use later to make filter settings in the report, appears in the column on the left. On the right are four manual links, which implement the following functions:

- Export to Excel
- Export to CSV
- Filter the report so that it only shows the results for calendar year 2002
- Filter the report for calendar year 2004

The first two functions (Export to Excel and Export to CSV) were implemented with SAP BW commands. The two filter functions were created using custom JavaScript functions, which generate and call a new URL.

Listing 6.1 shows the complete source code of the HTML view, which is essential for the migration of the web template.

```
<html>
<!-- BW data source object tags -->
<object>
  <param name="OWNER" value="SAP_BW"/>
  <param name="CMD" value="SET_DATA_PROVIDER"/>
  <param name="NAME" value="DATAPROVIDER_1"/>
  <param name="QUERY" value="ZJWRS_T10_2004"/>
  <param name="INFOCUBE" value="IC_RECHN"/>
  DATA_PROVIDER:             DATAPROVIDER_1
</object>

<object>
  <param name="OWNER" value="SAP_BW"/>
  <param name="CMD" value="SET_PROPERTIES"/>
  <param name="TEMPLATE_ID" value="ZJWRS_T10"/>
  <param name="SUPPRESS_SYSTEM_MESSAGES" value="X"/>
  <param name="SUPPRESS_WARNINGS" value="X"/>
  TEMPLATE PROPERTIES
</object>

<head>
  <meta name="GENERATOR" Content="Microsoft DHTML Editing Control">
  <title><SAP_BW_TEXT PROGRAM='ZBW_WEBREPORT_TEXTS'
                      KEY='001'></title>
```

```
  <link href="/sap/bw/Mime/BEx/StyleSheets/BWReports.css"
        type="text/css"
        rel="stylesheet"/>
<script language="JavaScript">
<!--
function filter(year) {
  var url = SAP_BW_URL_Get() + "&CMD=LDOC&TEMPLATE_ID=
            ZJWRS_T10&DATA_PROVIDER=DATAPROVIDER_1&
            FILTER_IOBJNM=0CALYEAR&FILTER_VALUE=" + year;
  //alert(url);
  SAPBWOpenURL(url);
}
//-->
</script>
</head>

<body bgcolor="#ffffff">
  <table border="0" width="600" bgcolor="#ffffff">
    <tr>
      <td valign="top" align="middle" bgcolor="#ddddff"
          colspan="2">
        <font style="FONT-WEIGHT: bold; FONT-SIZE: 18pt" >
          <SAP_BW_TEXT PROGRAM='ZBW_WEBREPORT_TEXTS'
                       KEY='001'></font>
      </td>
    </tr>
    <tr>
      <td colspan="2"> </td>
    </tr>
    <tr>
      <td colspan="2">
        <font style="FONT-SIZE: 9pt">
          This report displays the top 10 customers for
          the period you choose. You can use the
          navigation pane to narrow the
          results.
          <br><br>
          If you encounter any problems using the report,
          please contact the IT support hotline (555-1234)
          or write an e-mail to
          info@itsupport.de. We will contact you as
```

```
        soon as possible.
      </font>
     </td>
  </tr>
  <tr>
    <td colspan="2"> </td>
  </tr>
  <tr>
    <td valign="top" width="300">
      <object>
       <param name="OWNER" value="SAP_BW"/>
       <param name="CMD" value="GET_ITEM"/>
       <param name="NAME" value="NAVIGATIONBLOCK_1"/>
       <param name="ITEM_CLASS"
              value="CL_RSR_WWW_ITEM_NAV_BLOCK"/>
       <param name="DATA_PROVIDER" value="DATAPROVIDER_1"/>
       <param name="WIDTH" value="290"/>
       <param name="SHOW_EMPTY_SLICER" value="X"/>
       <param name="ITEM_NAV_BLOCK_IOBJNM_1" value="0CALYEAR"/>
       <param name="BOOKED_VALUES_1" value="Q"/>
       <param name="ITEM_NAV_BLOCK_IOBJNM_2" value="IO_KUNDE"/>
       <param name="BOOKED_VALUES_2" value="Q"/>
       <param name="ITEM_NAV_BLOCK_IOBJNM_3"
              value="IO_KUNDE__IO_ORT01"/>
       <param name="BOOKED_VALUES_3" value="Q"/>
       ITEM:            NAVIGATIONBLOCK_1
    </object>
    </td>
    <td valign="top" align="left" width="300">
      <table border="0" width="300">
        <tr>
          <td class="SAPBEXBorderFlexBoxTtl" width="290">
          Options:</td>
        </tr>
        <tr>
          <td valign="top" width="290">
            <A href="<SAP_BW_URL DATA_PROVIDER='DATAPROVIDER_1'
               CMD='EXPORT' FORMAT='XLS'>"><SAP_BW_TEXT
               PROGRAM='ZBW_WEBREPORT_TEXTS' KEY='002'>
            Excel</A><br>
            <A href="<SAP_BW_URL DATA_PROVIDER='DATAPROVIDER_1'
```

```
                CMD='EXPORT' FORMAT='CSV'>"><SAP_BW_TEXT
                PROGRAM='ZBW_WEBREPORT_TEXTS' KEY='002'>
              CSV</A><br>
              <A onclick="javascript:filter('2002')" href="#">
              <SAP_BW_TEXT PROGRAM='ZBW_WEBREPORT_TEXTS' KEY='003'>
              2002</A><br>
              <A onclick="javascript:filter('2004')" href="#">
              <SAP_BW_TEXT PROGRAM='ZBW_WEBREPORT_TEXTS' KEY='003'>
              2004</A>
            </td>
          </tr>
        </table>
      </td>
    </tr>
    <tr>
      <td valign="top" colspan="2">
        <object>
          <param name="OWNER" value="SAP_BW"/>
          <param name="CMD" value="GET_ITEM"/>
          <param name="NAME" value="TABLE_1"/>
          <param name="ITEM_CLASS" value="CL_RSR_WWW_ITEM_GRID"/>
          <param name="DATA_PROVIDER" value="DATAPROVIDER_1"/>
          <param name="CAPTION" value="Data"/>
          <param name="WIDTH" value="600"/>
          ITEM:            TABLE_1
        </object>
      </td>
    </tr>
  </table>
</body>
</html>
```

Listing 6.1 Source Code of the ZJWRS_T10 Web Template

The web template consists of various special features, which are described next.

At the start of the template, you'll see a JavaScript area containing the `filter(year)` function. This function creates a new URL based on the `year` input parameter. This URL is then called via `SAPBWOpenURL()`. The function is used in the options area and filters the results for the years 2002 and 2004.

Next, a <SAP_BW_TEXT> command is used to display the header of the web template. This command enables access to text elements in an ABAP program, for example, to ensure that texts can be displayed in multiple languages. The command requires the following two parameters:

- **The PROGRAM parameter**
  The name of the ABAP program in the SAP BW system.
- **The KEY parameter**
  The three-digit key of the text element.

In our example, the ABAP program is called ZBW_WEBREPORT_TEXTS and has three text elements (see Figure 6.15), which have also been translated.

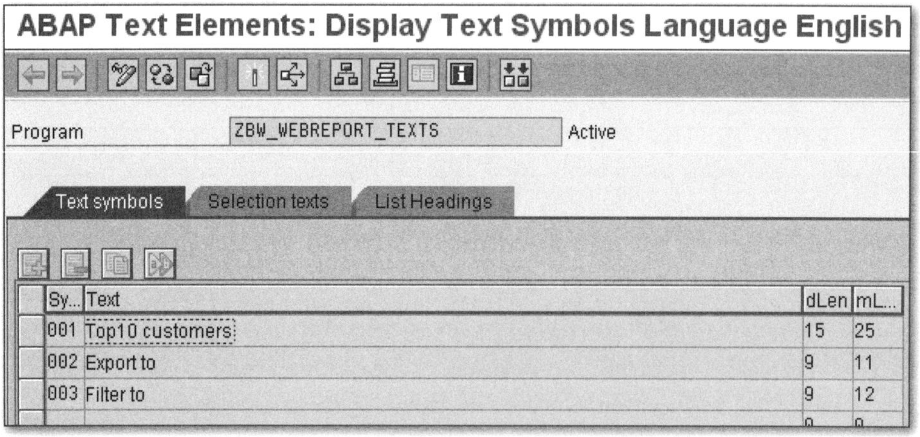

Figure 6.15 Text Elements in the ZBW_WEBREPORTS_TEXTS ABAP Program

The header is followed by standard text, which is formatted using CSS statements. Below this text is a table with two columns. The column on the left contains a generic navigation block, which can filter the three characteristics of calendar year, customer, and city. Various commands for filtering and exporting have been entered in the column on the right:

- **Export to Excel and CSV**
  The <SAP_BW_URL> command allows you to perform an export. This command requires the `DATA_PROVIDER` (specifies the content to be accessed by the com-

mand), CMD (the command to be used for the DataProvider), and FORMAT (the export format) parameters. In our example, these are DATAPROVIDER_1 with the EXPORT command and XLS or CSV format.

- **Filter by calendar year**
  The filter(year) JavaScript function is used here to filter the results according to the preceding logic. The <SAP_BW_TEXT> command is used again to display the text that is to be output.

A particular feature of the display in the column on the right should be pointed out at this point. The SAPBEXBorderFlexBoxTtl CSS class was used here. This is an SAP BW standard CSS class, which is used, for example, to display the title of generic navigation blocks. It has been used in this case to adapt the layout of the options area to the layout of the navigation block and to demonstrate how the CSS classes have changed in the new release.

Finally, at the bottom of the screen, you'll see the query from the last section displayed in the form of a table.

The following functions have thus been implemented in a web template and must be checked after the migration and corrected manually if required:

- According to SAP, the generic navigation block used is not automatically migrated.
- To display two languages, texts were read from an ABAP program using the <SAP_BW_TEXT> command.
- Excel export functions were implemented with the <SAP_BW_URL> command.
- The display of the options area in the column on the right is based on the SAPBEXBorderFlexBoxTtl CSS class, which must be checked for errors after the migration.
- A custom JavaScript function was used to implement filtering based on the calendar year characteristic (results restricted to 2002 and 2004).

Finally, warning and error messages were suppressed. The web template called is shown on the Web in Figure 6.16. Our objective is now to create exactly the same layout with a 7.0 web template.

Figure 6.16 Web Layout of the 3.5 Web Template

6.4.2 Migrating the Web Templates

In the new Web Application Designer, you start migration of the web template by selecting the menu option EXTRAS • MIGRATION TOOL. First, you are shown an overview of the individual steps involved in the process (see Figure 6.17).

The first step is to select the web template to be migrated. Next, you can decide whether the conversion to XML is to be automatic or manual. Automatic conversion is selected here in our example. After you select the web template, you can start the conversion process (see Figure 6.18).

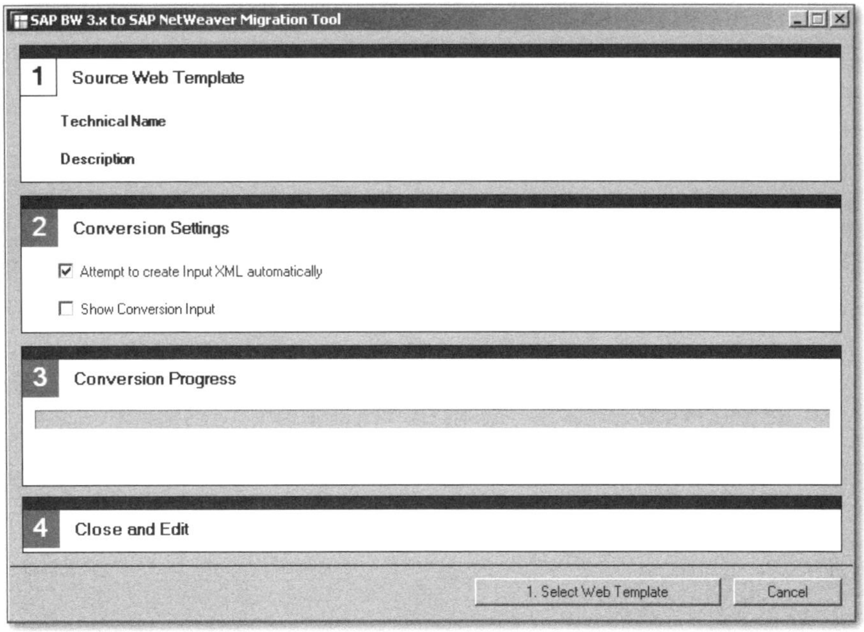

Figure 6.17 The Migration Tool in SAP NetWeaver BI

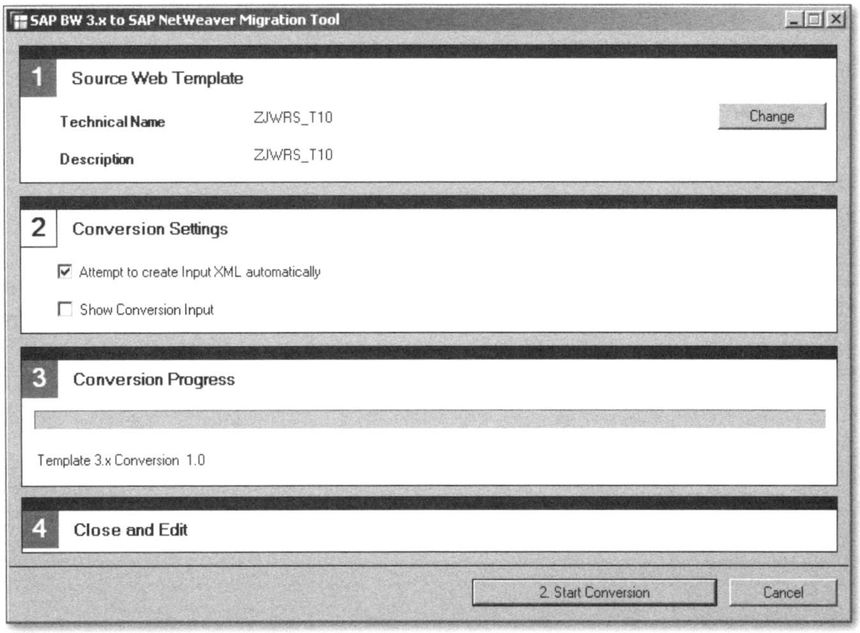

Figure 6.18 Migration Tool Complete with Details for Starting the Conversion

After conversion is started in our example, a critical message appears relatively quickly, which, at first glance, is rather confusing. The message indicates an application error (see Figure 6.19).

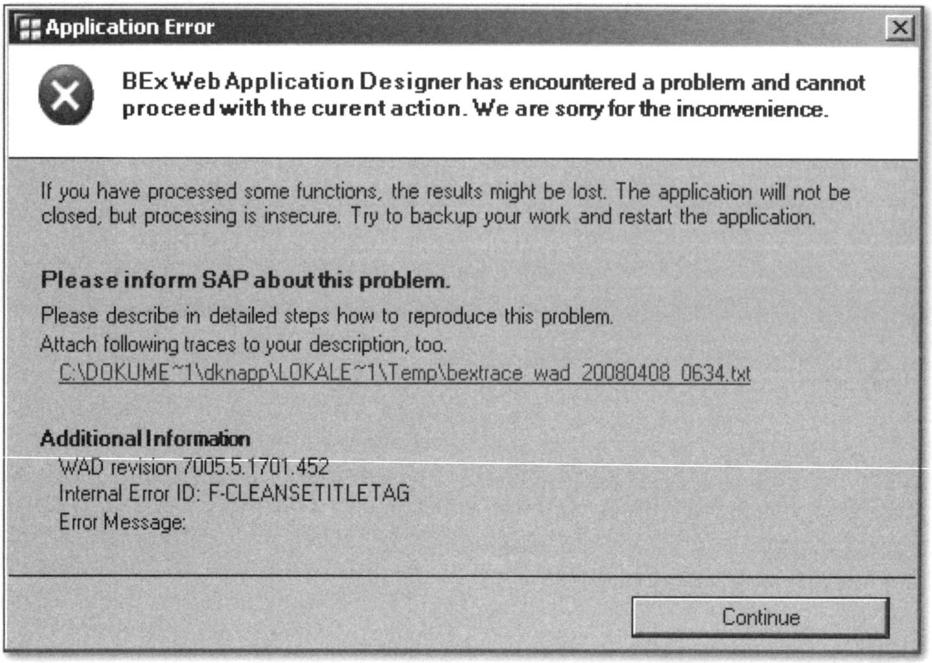

Figure 6.19 Application Error After Conversion Starts

On closer examination, however, you'll see that the migration tool has detected a problem with the conversion to XML, as can be seen in the trace file. The following text appears at the very top of this file: "TRACE FAIL how on earth can the string contain only an opening TITLE tag, and not a closing one as well?" (looks like even developers like to have a little fun sometimes!). This indicates problems with the `<title>` tag, which we'll return to later.

After you confirm this "application error," the migration continues and ends with the overview shown in Figure 6.20.

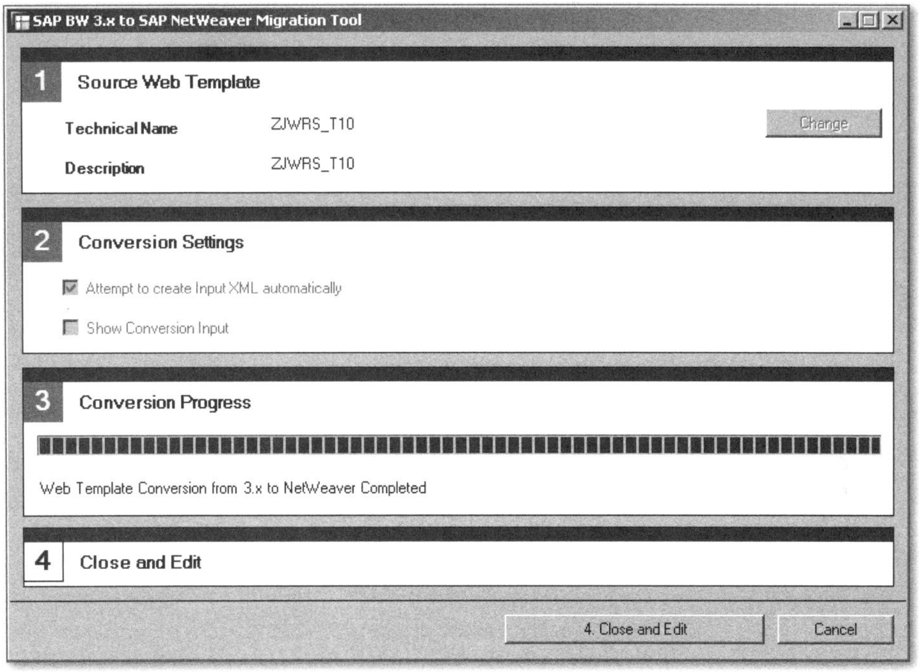

Figure 6.20 End of the Conversion Process During the Migration

The migrated web template then appears in the XHTML view. Listing 6.2 shows the complete source code after the migration.

```
<bi:bisp xmlns="http://www.w3.org/TR/REC-html40"
    xmlns:bi="http://xml.sap.com/2005/01/bi/wad/bisp"
    xmlns:jsp="http://java.sun.com/JSP/Page" >
<html >
  <head >
    <title >
<!-- BW data source object tags -->
      <bi:text program="ZBW_WEBREPORT_TEXTS" key="001" />
    </title>

    <link href="bwmimerep:///sap/bw/mime//BEx/StyleSheets/
                BWReports.css"
          type="text/css" rel="stylesheet" />
    <meta http-equiv="Content-Type" content="text/html;
          charset=utf-8" />
  </head>
  <body bgcolor="#ffffff" >
```

```
<bi:QUERY_VIEW_DATA_PROVIDER name="DATAPROVIDER_1" >
  <bi:INITIAL_STATE value="QUERY" >
    <bi:QUERY value="ZJWRS_T10_2004" />
  </bi:INITIAL_STATE>
</bi:QUERY_VIEW_DATA_PROVIDER>
<bi:TEMPLATE_PARAMETERS name="TEMPLATE_PARAMETERS_1" >
  <bi:WARNINGS_VISIBLE value="" />
  <bi:SYSTEM_MESSAGES_VISIBLE value="" />
</bi:TEMPLATE_PARAMETERS>
<table width="600" bgcolor="#ffffff" border="0" >
  <tbody >
    <tr >
      <td valign="top" align="middle" bgcolor="#ddddff"
          colspan="2" >
        <font style="FONT-WEIGHT: bold; FONT-SIZE: 18pt"
         [SAP_BW_TEXT:_x0020_PROGRAM_x003D__x0022__x0027_
         ZBW_WEBREPORT_TEXTS_x0027__x0022__x0020_KEY_x003D_
         _x0022
         __x0027_001_x0027_:SAP_BW_TEXT]&lt;&quot;/font&gt;
        </font>
      </td>
    </tr>
    <tr >
      <td colspan="2" />
    </tr>
    <tr >
      <td colspan="2" >
        <font style="FONT-SIZE: 9pt" >
      This report displays the top 10 customers for
      the period you choose. You can use the
      navigation pane to narrow the
      results.
      <br><br>
      If you encounter any problems using the report,
      please contact the IT support hotline (555-1234)
      or write an e-mail to
      info@itsupport.de. We will contact you as
      soon as possible.
        </font>
      </td>
    </tr>
    <tr >
      <td colspan="2" />
```

```
</tr>
<tr >
  <td valign="top" width="300" >
    <bi:NAVIGATION_PANE_ITEM name="NAVIGATIONBLOCK_1"
        designheight="300" designwidth="290" >
      <bi:WIDTH value="290" />
      <bi:WITH_TRAY value="X" type="CHOICE" >
        <bi:TRAY_SETTINGS type="COMPOSITE" >
          <bi:CAPTION_VISIBLE value="X" />
        </bi:TRAY_SETTINGS>
      </bi:WITH_TRAY>
      <bi:DATA_PROVIDER_REF value="DATAPROVIDER_1" />
      <bi:FILTERING_ENABLED value="X" />
      <bi:NAVIGATION_BLOCK_CONTENT value="QUERYVIEW" />
    </bi:NAVIGATION_PANE_ITEM>
  </td>
  <td valign="top" align="left" width="300" >
    <table width="300" border="0" >
      <tbody >
        <tr >
          <td class="SAPBEXBorderFlexBoxTtl" width="290">
            Options:</td>
        </tr>
        <tr >
          <td valign="top" width="290" >
            <a >
              <bi:attribute name="href" >
                <bi:EXPORT >
                  <bi:EXPORT_FORMAT value="XLS" />
                </bi:EXPORT>
              </bi:attribute>
              <bi:text program="ZBW_WEBREPORT_TEXTS"
                       key="002" />
            </a>
            <br />
              <a >
                <bi:attribute name="href" >
                  <bi:EXPORT >
                    <bi:EXPORT_FORMAT value="CSV" />
                  </bi:EXPORT>
                </bi:attribute>
                <bi:text program="ZBW_WEBREPORT_TEXTS"
                         key="002" />
```

```
                        </a>
                        <br />
                        <a onclick="javascript:filter(&apos;2002
                        &apos;)"
                           href="#" >[SAP_BW_TEXT:_x0020_PROGRAM_
                                     x003D__x0022__x0027_ZBW_
                                     WEBREPORT_TEXTS_x0027__x0022_
                                     _x0020_KEY_x003D__x0027_003_
                                     x0027_:SAP_BW_TEXT] 2002
                        </a>
                        <br />
                        <a onclick="javascript:filter(&apos;2004
                                    &apos;)"
                           href="#" >
                           [SAP_BW_TEXT:_x0020_PROGRAM_x003D
                           __x0022__x0027_ZBW_WEBREPORT_TEXTS_x0027
                           __x0022__x0020_KEY_x003D__x0027_003_x0027
                           _:SAP_BW_TEXT] 2004
                        </a>
                      </td>
                    </tr>
                  </tbody>
                </table>
              </td>
            </tr>
            <tr >
              <td valign="top" colspan="2" >
                <bi:ANALYSIS_ITEM name="TABLE_1" designheight="300"
                    designwidth="600" >
                  <bi:WIDTH value="600" />
                  <bi:WITH_TRAY value="X" type="CHOICE" >
                    <bi:TRAY_SETTINGS type="COMPOSITE" >
                      <bi:CAPTION value="Data" />
                      <bi:CAPTION_VISIBLE value="X" />
                    </bi:TRAY_SETTINGS>
                  </bi:WITH_TRAY>
                  <bi:DATA_PROVIDER_REF value="DATAPROVIDER_1" />
                </bi:ANALYSIS_ITEM>
              </td>
            </tr>
          </tbody>
        </table>
        <bi:SCRIPT_ITEM name="MIGRATED_JAVASCRIPT_ITEM"
```

```
            designheight="50" designwidth="100" >
          <bi:SCRIPT_CONTENT_TYPE_LIST value="JAVASCRIPT" />
          <bi:SCRIPT value="biLargeData:B6ZMIDYA98WWEXI0BCC7B170W" />
        </bi:SCRIPT_ITEM>
      </body>
    </html>
</bi:bisp>
```

Listing 6.2 XHTML Source Code After Migration of the Web Template

As you can see, the migration tool does not convert all custom HTML tags correctly. Instead, it always inserts a blank space before the closing ">" symbol. This produces the application error during migration, which occurs again during the syntax check:

- Closing tag `</title>` before `<bi:text>` is missing.
- Unexpected `</title>` tag is removed.
- The `align` attribute of the `<td>` tag contains the invalid value `middle`.

All of these messages are warning messages rather than error messages, and you should therefore correct the errors. The first two error messages are produced by the application error. In this case, the migration tool detected a blank space in the `<title >` tag and was unable to find the closing tag. However, removing the blank space does not eliminate the error, and the error message is still displayed.

This error message occurs because the `<title>` tag must not contain any SAP BW commands in SAP NetWeaver BI. The error message only disappears after you remove the command.

After you correct the `<title>` tag, you must also correct the incorrect `middle` value in the `align` attribute. As you can see from Listing 6.2, the source code did not contain this value before the migration. To correct the value, replace it with `center`. After you do this, all warning messages disappear, and the web template is now syntactically correct.

Note

In the example provided here, the `center` value is replaced with `middle` again after switching from the XHTML view to the layout view. This produces a new error message. This appears to be an application error.

However, the web template is still not fully functional because the migration tool was unable to convert all modules correctly. For example, the JavaScript part no longer exists in the header area, and some SAP BW commands appear in an unusual green format (see circled area in Figure 6.21).

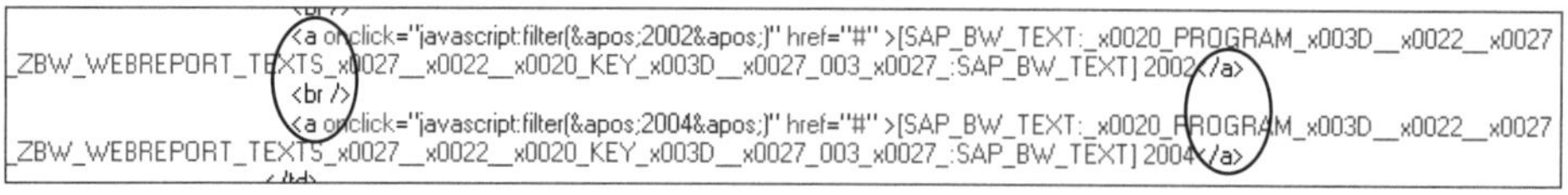

Figure 6.21 Migrated SAP_BW_TEXT Commands

You must correct this formatting manually because the tool was unable to convert it. All remaining corrections to be made to the web template are discussed in the next section.

6.4.3 Correcting SAP_BW_TEXT Commands

The <SAP_BW_TEXT> commands were replaced with <bi:text> commands (see the following box).

The SAP_BW_TEXT Command in SAP NetWeaver BI

The <SAP_BW_TEXT> command for reading text elements from an ABAP program was replaced in SAP NetWeaver BI with an XHTML <bi:text> command, which comprises the same PROGRAM and KEY parameters. Thus, <SAP_BW_TEXT PROGRAM='A' KEY='001'> in SAP BW becomes <bi:text program='A' key='001'/> in SAP NetWeaver BI.

Therefore, correct all <SAP_BW_TEXT> macros in green formatting (refer to Figure 6.21) with the corresponding <bi:text> commands, as illustrated here by the example of the title:

- **Old source code**

```
[SAP_BW_TEXT:_x0020_PROGRAM_x003D__x0022__x0027_ZBW_WEBREPORT_TEXTS_
x0027__x0022__x0020_KEY_x003D__x0022__x0027_001_x0027_:SAP_BW_
TEXT]&lt;&quot;/font&gt;
```

- **New source code**

```
<bi:text program='ZBW_WEBREPORT_TEXTS' KEY='001'/>
```

Do the same with the two filter commands from the options area.

Caution

You need to check all <SAP_BW_TEXT> commands that appear at first glance to have been correctly translated. In our example, a subtle error managed to slip through. Although the migration tool generated correct <bi:text> commands for the export command, it deleted the word "Excel" or "CSV" from the description. As a result, the finished web template would contain the incomplete phrase "Export to"!

6.4.4 Correcting the JavaScript Statements

The JavaScript area initially appears to have disappeared. The migration tool has, however, recognized this area and transferred it into the relevant web item, namely, Script. You will find the Script web item at the very end of the source code (see Listing 6.3).

```
<bi:SCRIPT_ITEM name="MIGRATED_JAVASCRIPT_ITEM"
    designheight="50" designwidth="100" >
  <bi:SCRIPT_CONTENT_TYPE_LIST value="JAVASCRIPT" />
  <bi:SCRIPT value="biLargeData:B6ZMIDYA98WWEXI0BCC7B170W" />
</bi:SCRIPT_ITEM>
```

Listing 6.3 Migrated JavaScript Source Code

This is a key difference between SAP BW 3.5 and SAP NetWeaver BI within the Web Application Designer. JavaScript source code can only be used in the Script web item and is no longer displayed in the HTML or XHTML view.

To display and change the source text, right-click on the Script item and select the Edit SCRIPT_ITEM option (see Figure 6.22). This also works in the XHTML view.

Figure 6.22 Editing the SCRIPT_ITEM for Displaying the JavaScript Source Code

This opens a window in which the source code is displayed.

This was automatically commented out after the migration. If you want to use it again, you must remove the comment, as instructed by the text generated for the JavaScript (see Figure 6.23).

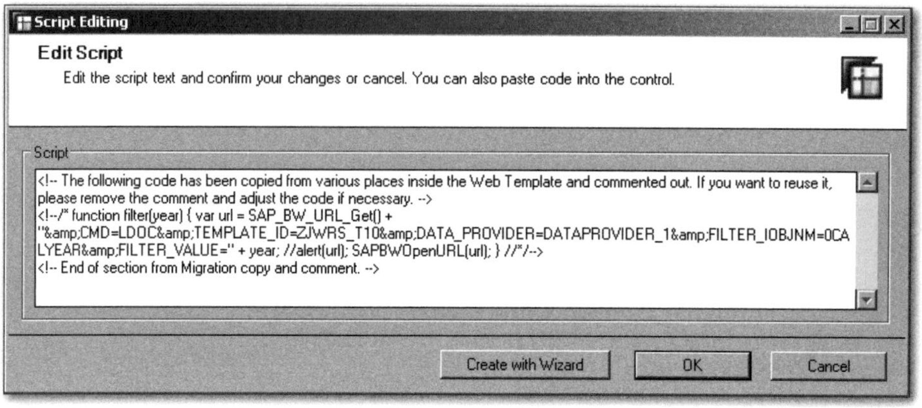

Figure 6.23 Editing the JavaScript Source Code After Migration

The commenting out of the source code by the migration tool is a useful feature because the source code would otherwise no longer be functional after the migration. In addition to the JavaScript functions used, the entire syntax for passing parameters within the URL has thus also changed. The URL can now be considered to be a portal URL and no longer an SAP BW URL. Accordingly, a different server with different parameters is called.

The correction of this simple, two-line JavaScript function has suddenly become quite a complicated task. If you want to reuse this function, you must follow these two steps:

1. Create a JavaScript statement with the Script Wizard, which performs filtering.
2. Remove the old `<a>` tags and replace them with the new `LINK_ITEM` web items (in the WEB ITEMS • VARIOUS • LINK area).
3. Link the JavaScript function created with the Script Wizard in Point 1 to the new `LINK_ITEM` (the end result is that the `LINK_ITEM` becomes a `<a>` tag).

These steps are demonstrated in the next section, using the example of the old `filter(year)` function, which performed filtering by calendar year (i.e., 2002 and 2004) for the 0CALYEAR characteristic.

6.4.5 Creating a JavaScript-Statement with the Wizard

First, use the wizard to create a JavaScript statement. You can use the existing SCRIPT web item for this purpose. Right-click to open it for editing. Then delete the migrated source code and choose CREATE WITH WIZARD. This opens a view, where you can select a command from a list. In our example, you need the SET_SELECTION_STATE_SIMPLE command, which you'll find under COMMANDS FOR DATA PROVIDER • DATA PROVIDER COMMANDS FOR FILTER VALUES • SET FILTER VALUE FOR A CHARACTERISTIC in the menu (see Figure 6.24).

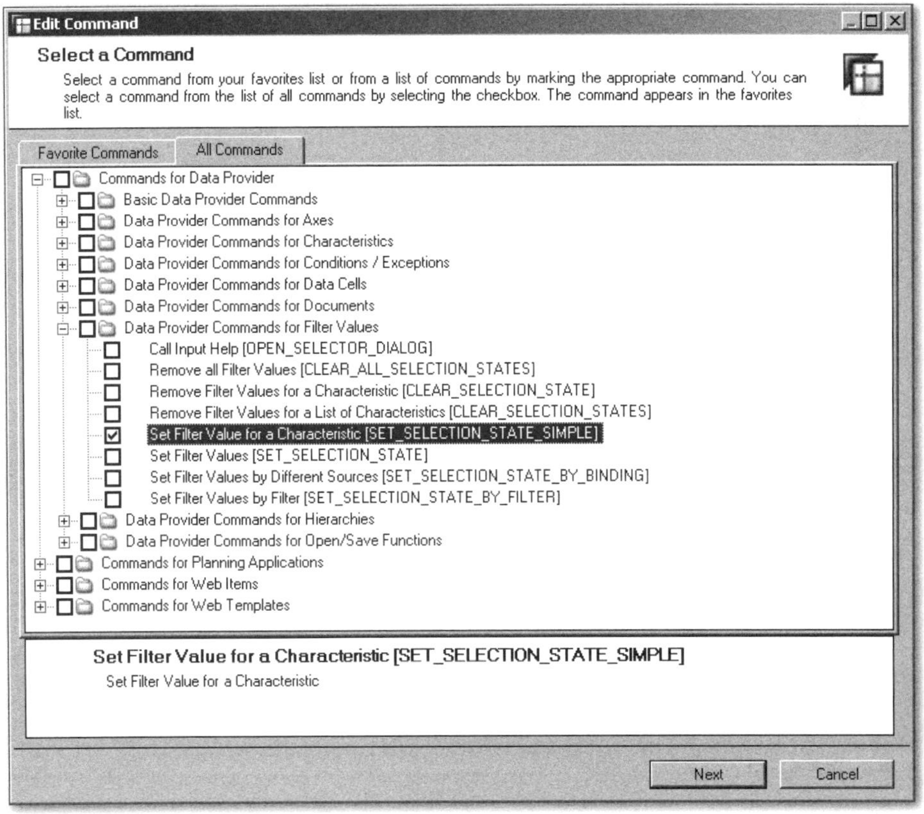

Figure 6.24 Selecting the SET_SELECTION_STATE_SIMPLE Function for Filtering Characteristics

Click on Next to select the DataProvider for which you want to use the command. In our example, this is the DATAPROVIDER_1 DataProvider. When you confirm the selection, a view opens, where you can select the characteristic you want to filter. Here, select the 0CALYEAR characteristic, and set the filter value to 2004, for example (see Figure 6.25).

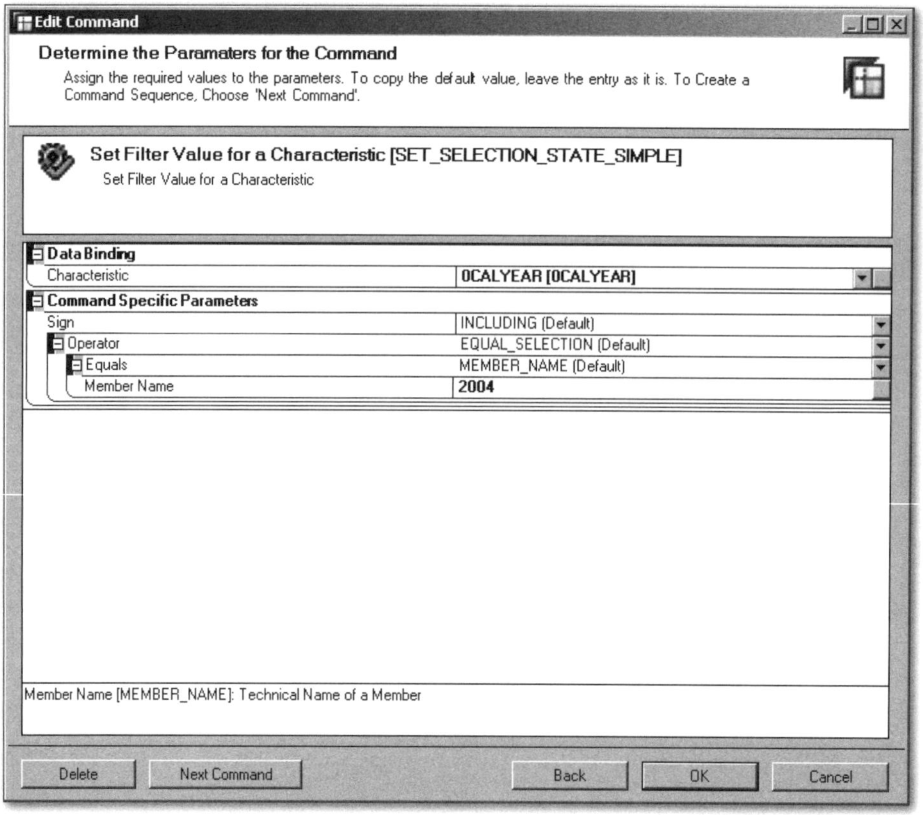

Figure 6.25 Editing the Command and Selecting the Characteristic to be Filtered

You have now created a JavaScript filtering function. As you can tell from the source code, the Script web item requires 73 lines for this function. You can now use this script to incorporate the filter into a `LINK_ITEM`.

6.4.6 Creating and Editing a LINK_ITEM Web Item

First, delete the old `<a>` tags, which no longer work correctly. Then select (see above) the `LINK_ITEM` web item and insert it at the position previously occupied by the `<a>` statement. Next, you need to modify the behavior of the application and implement the JavaScript function you have just created (see Figure 6.26).

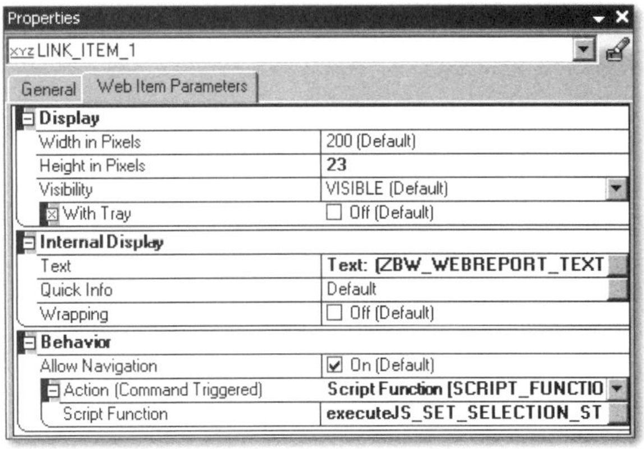

Figure 6.26 Implementing the JavaScript Function in the LINK_ITEM Web Item

Remember to use the text for the link (under Internal Display). You also have the option of using an ABAP program to find and display the text, although this is now an outdated approach (see Figure 6.27). However, this is irrelevant for the migration because the sole objective of the first step is to ensure that the new web template is functional.

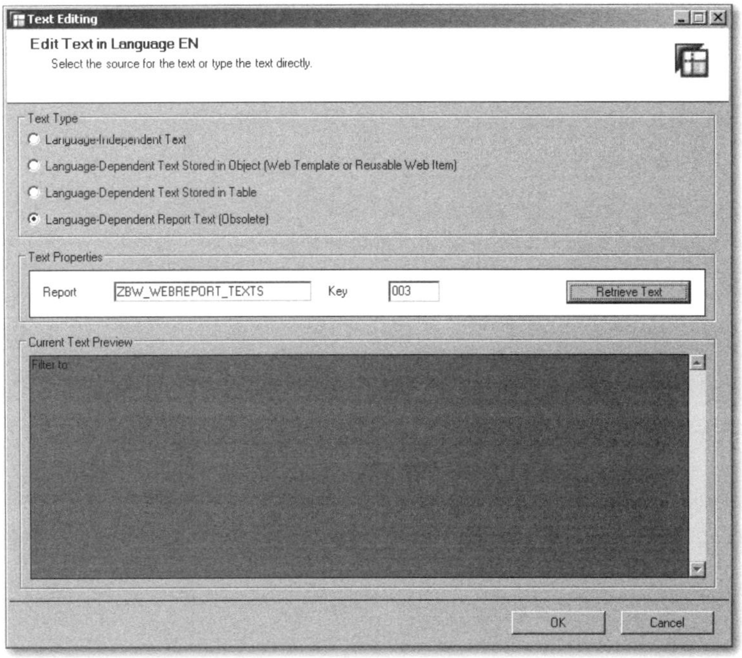

Figure 6.27 Selecting the Report and the Text Element to Display the Text

You can also customize this text, for example, by adding "2002" and "2004". However, you must do this in the XHTML view because it is not possible to access the source code from the properties view. Listing 6.4 shows a complete LINK_ITEM from the XHTML view:

```
<bi:LINK_ITEM name="LINK_ITEM_1" designheight="23"
designwidth="200" >
  <bi:HEIGHT value="23" />
  <bi:TEXT_CONTENT value="Text: (ZBW_WEBREPORT_TEXTS-003) 2002" >
    <bi:text program="ZBW_WEBREPORT_TEXTS" key="003" /> 2002
  </bi:TEXT_CONTENT>
  <bi:ACTION type="CHOICE" value="SCRIPT_FUNCTION" >
    <bi:SCRIPT_FUNCTION value=
"executeJS_SET_SELECTION_STATE_SIMPLE_R2002"/>
  </bi:ACTION>
</bi:LINK_ITEM>
```

Listing 6.4 Source Code of LINK_ITEM_1

Follow the same steps for filtering by the value "2002", that is, create a new JavaScript function and link it to a second LINK_ITEM. The result is shown in Figure 6.28.

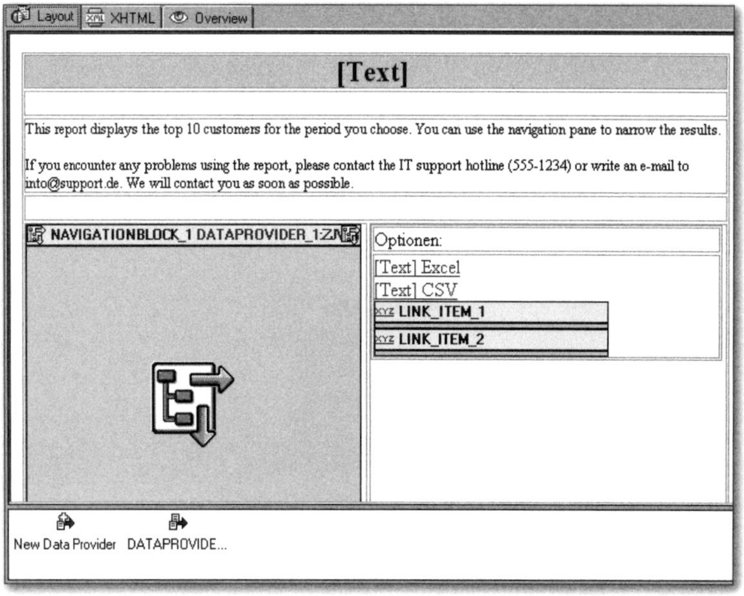

Figure 6.28 Layout View After Positioning of Both LINK_ITEMs

You can use the same technical name when saving the web template. As a result, a new 7.0 version of the old SAP BW 3.5 object is created. Meanwhile, the old object continues to exist and is still functional.

6.4.7 Calling the Web Template for the First Time

Now that the migration is finished, the next step is to call your web template for the first time and view the result. The web template is now fully functional. Figure 6.29 shows the result of the first call of the web template.

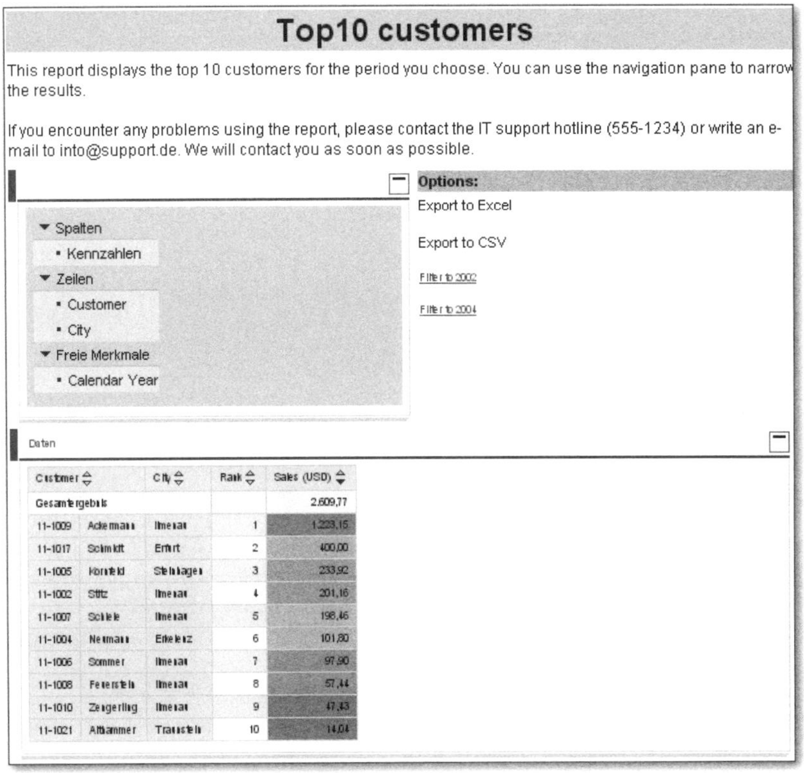

Figure 6.29 First Call of the Edited Web Template

However, the results are disappointing because the layout differs from SAP BW 3.5 and is not what we were expecting. For example, all fonts used in the web items are several sizes too small. You'll also notice that the interface has been adjusted to the Portal layout in SAP NetWeaver BI. As a result, web items are always displayed in an iView, where they can be expanded or collapsed as required (tray). The layout of the SAPBEXBorderFlexBoxTtl CSS class, which was used in the old version and was incorporated into the Options area, still works in the new version but is out of sync with the rest of the layout.

6.4.8 Initial Conclusions

Even though functionality has been replicated, the layout is not fit to be presented to customers. Therefore, the functional migration, after which the web template is functional once more, is usually followed by a migration of the layout (optical migration).

6.4.9 Optical Migration

You can see the first results of optical migration immediately by deleting the old SAP BW style sheet from the XHTML view (see Listing 6.5).

```
<link href="bwmimerep:///sap/bw/mime//BEx/StyleSheets/BWReports.css"
      type="text/css" rel="stylesheet" />
```

Listing 6.5 Removing the Old SAP BW Style Sheet

After you do this, the new style sheet is used instead, which displays the correct font sizes.

As you can see in Figure 6.30, removing the style sheet produces a much-improved layout. Note that all manually used CSS formats are replaced by unformatted text.

Caution

If you've used CSS formats from the old style sheet, these are replaced with normal text after you remove the style sheet. The greater the number of CSS formats you used in the old style sheet, the greater the number of changes to be made.

The final change to be made for our sample web template is the modification of the Options area, in which the SAPBEXBorderFlexBoxTtl CSS class has been used. You can, for example, use a GROUP_ITEM element for this purpose. This has a tray that adapts the layout to the navigation block.

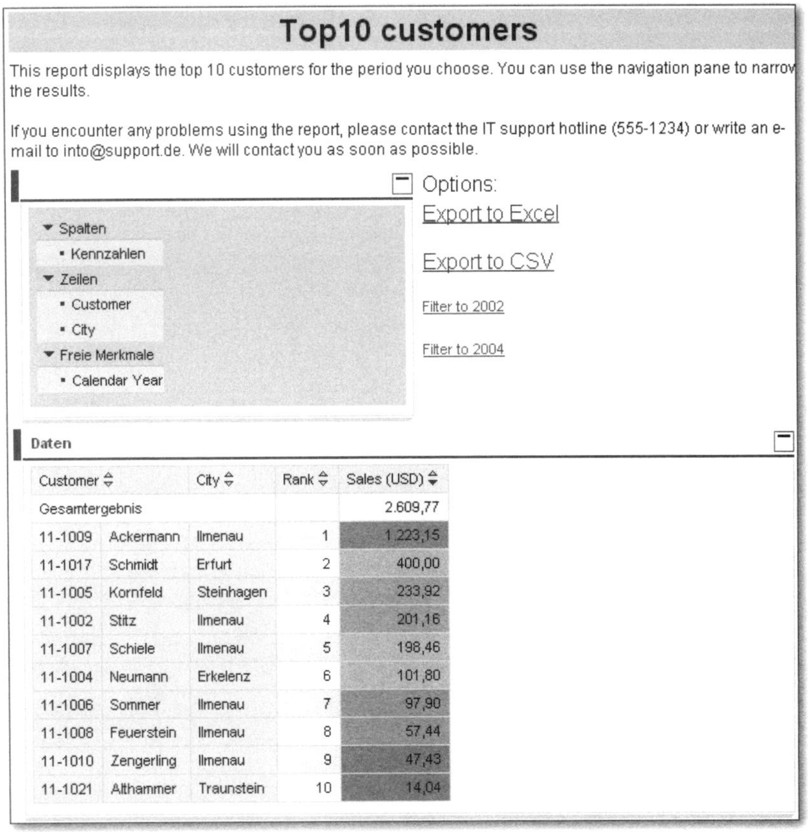

Figure 6.30 Layout After Removing the Old SAP BW Style Sheet

6.4.10 Conclusion

In this section, you've learned how to migrate a very simple web template, and you've seen the changes that need to be made as a result of the migration. In addition, you've learned that the migration of a web template comprises both a functional and an optical migration. Functional migration restores functionality, whereas optical migration redesigns the display.

The following section discusses in detail the special considerations to be made in relation to the migration.

6.5 Special Considerations When Performing a Migration

The first point to note is the fact, mentioned previously, that the web template migration comprises both a concept migration and an optical migration. Depending on the complexity of the functions and the layout, both migrations may be very time-consuming, particularly if you are not sure how or even if the old functionality will be mapped in the new release.

This section deals with functions that can be implemented without any problem in SAP BW 3.5 but cannot be implemented in SAP NetWeaver, at least at first glance.

6.5.1 Table Interface

The first function for which there is unfortunately no equivalent in SAP NetWeaver BI is the *table interface* from the Web Design API for tables. The table interface was a practical way to modify or extend tables and navigation blocks on the web using methods in a special ABAP class.

To do this, you created a class that inherited from the CL_RSR_WWW_MODIFY_TABLE class in Transaction SE24 in the back end. The class methods had to be redefined to modify rows and columns in a table or navigation block from the Web Application Designer. You then had to define the resulting class in the TABLE INTERFACE CLASS parameter in a table or a navigation block (see Figure 6.31).

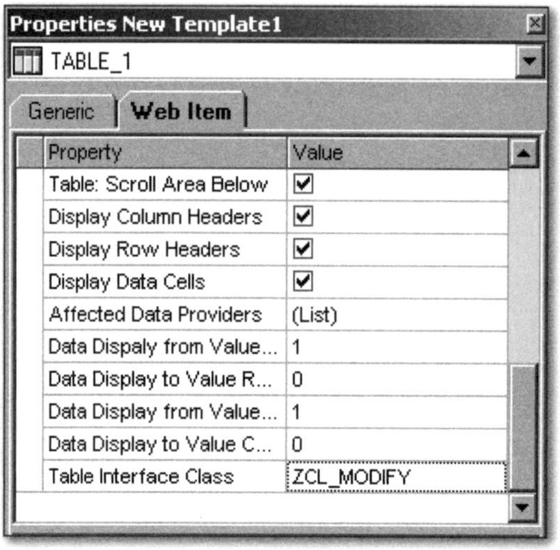

Figure 6.31 Defining a Table Interface Class for a "Table" Web Item

This function doesn't exist in SAP NetWeaver BI. According to SAP, there are no plans to make the function available again in the future (see Release Notes for SAP NetWeaver 7.0). The reason for this has to do with the relocation of reporting to the SAP NetWeaver Portal. You can therefore expect to encounter restrictions in reporting if you've been using the table interface.

In some cases, the table interface was also used in SAP BW where it allowed functions to be implemented faster than with the dedicated options provided. A good example of this is the display of documents using characteristic values. The table interface was very frequently used to display documents or related information by clicking on certain characteristic values. The same can be done, in a slightly more complicated fashion, using the document management functionality in Knowledge Management (see Appendix A, Bibliography).

6.5.2 Using JavaScript

As you've seen in the last section, you can still use JavaScript, but it has become more complicated to do so. For example, due to XHTML compatibility, it's no longer possible to have `<script>` areas in the header area of the web template. Instead, you must place each JavaScript function within a Script web item.

However, this has no impact on functionality because it is only the storage location that has changed. You can still access JavaScript functions in the attributes of HTML tags, as shown in Listing 6.6.

```
<body onload="javascript:function(param1, param2)">
[...]
</body>
```

Listing 6.6 Example of the Use of a JavaScript

Therefore, the conversion of JavaScript statements, rather than their storage location, results in the necessary modifications. Many functions are no longer supported, for example, the `SAPBWOpenURL()` and `SAP_BW_URL_Get()` functions, which were required to create and call URLs. This is due to the relocation of reporting to the SAP NetWeaver Portal.

We use JavaScript frequently in SAP BW 3.5 to create new, dynamic URLS, for example, for changing a DataProvider or for filtering. This produced statement blocks with upwards of 200 lines of source code, which made the migration much more difficult later on. These functions then had to be translated into the new "language" of SAP NetWeaver BI.

6.5.3 Using SAP BW Commands

SAP BW commands are commands that you could use in the Web Application Designer. They allowed you to perform filtering, drill-downs, sorting, and exports. You could also use these commands to add text contained in text elements from ABAP programs.

These SAP BW commands are no longer available. However, they have been converted into new commands and can be used in their new, changed form. Practically all of the SAP BW commands you would have used have been replaced with new commands in the migration tool. For example, we saw earlier how the export to Excel and CSV has been converted:

- **SAP BW command**

```
<SAP_BW_URL DATA_PROVIDER='DATAPROVIDER_1'
            CMD='EXPORT' FORMAT='XLS'>
```

- **Corresponding command in SAP NetWeaver BI**

```
<bi:EXPORT>
  <bi:EXPORT_FORMAT value="XLS" />
</bi:EXPORT>
```

We also saw how the <SAP_BW_TEXT> command has been replaced with a <bi:text> statement.

- **SAP BW command**

```
<SAP_BW_TEXT PROGRAM='A' KEY='001'>
```

- **Corresponding command in SAP NetWeaver BI**

```
<bi:TEXT PROGRAM='A' KEY='001' />
```

It would go beyond the scope of this book to provide a list of all the new commands that correspond to the old SAP BW commands. However, you can refer to the SAP Library, where you'll find an example of each new command.

The next section provides practical recommendations for performing a migration and methods for estimating the cost of migration.

SAP Library

The SAP Library is available online at *http://help.sap.com*. From there, you can navigate to the SAP Library documentation for SAP NetWeaver and select the SAP NetWeaver 7.0 Library. Then drill down as follows to display an overview of the new commands: SAP NetWeaver Library • SAP NetWeaver by Key Capability • Information Integration: Key Areas • Business Intelligence • BI Suite: Business Explorer • BEx Web • Web Application Design: BEx Web Application Designer • Web Design API • Commands. Alternatively, use the following link: *http://help.sap.com/saphelp_nw70/helpdata/en/71/8a784226d1d242e10000000a1550b0/content.htm*.

6.6 Recommendations for Your Migration Project

Although the web template you migrated earlier was a very simple one, you can already tell how complicated a task migration may become in the area of web reporting. Therefore, it's very important to perform a thorough check to determine whether a migration actually makes sense in your specific situation. A full list of recommendations for performing the migration is provided next.

6.6.1 Recommendations

Determining the effects of a migration before you perform one is absolutely vital.

In practice, we have often encountered a problem directly related to the relocation of reporting to the SAP NetWeaver Portal.

Recommendation 1: Necessity of the Migration

Because reports can be migrated independently of other reports, you need to determine exactly which reports are to be migrated and which are not. Note also that all new reports are displayed with the SAP NetWeaver Portal, which means that all URLs will change. Therefore, it's very important to determine the effects of migration on other applications that interact with the BI system (see the following brief case study).

Case Study

If you want to use the new functions in SAP NetWeaver BI, you need the SAP NetWeaver Portal, which was not available in release SAP BW 3.5. For this reason, we developed a customized portal for one customer based on a BSP application, in which reports could be displayed via URL.

The portal we developed was extremely dynamic; for example, the technical name of a report was sufficient to display it. When it came to migrating a report, we had to consider what to do in relation to the customer-specific portal. Our options were as follows:

- Continue to use the existing portal and convert the dynamic to the new reporting functionality.
- Rebuild the customer-specific portal in the new SAP NetWeaver Portal.

Both options are conceivable and plausible. However, the best option is to redesign the portal with the SAP NetWeaver Portal, which will continue to be viable in the future and will allow for parallel operation.

If you decide that the migration is essential, for example, because you want to use new functions that are not available in SAP BW, it's still advisable *not* to migrate queries.

Recommendation 2: Migration of Queries

Because you can use a 3.5 query in a 7.0 web template without any problems, 3.5 queries should not be migrated. A query is thus upward compatible but not downward compatible. After you save a 3.5 query in BEx Query Designer 7.0, it can no longer be used in the older version.

Use of the BEx Report Designer, for example, to create DIN A4 formats for your report, is not a valid reason to perform a migration. A report may be based on a 3.5 query, and it's also possible to define a (predefined) portal URL of a report in an old 3.5 web application to create PDF reports.

Recommendation 3: Migration of Web Templates

Careful consideration must also be applied to the migration of web templates. First, determine whether the migration will add value. Reflect on the complexity of your report in answering this question. You should only migrate a web template if it will add value.

Of course, these recommendations are only relevant if you exert a certain influence over the decision-making process in your company, for example, if you are an internal or external consultant. If the company has already decided in favor of a complete migration, all of the preceding cautionary notes are irrelevant.

In such a case, it's all the more important to estimate the amount of effort involved and to work out a plan for the migration. You should perform a migration of thc reporting area as specified next.

Recommendation 4: Complete Migration of the Reporting Area

You should always begin this migration with one or two individual reports in the development system and have these approved by the business department in the test system after they have been migrated. Choose a very simple report and a very complex test case, based on the interaction and the source code. This will give you a good feeling of how much time and effort should be allocated to the migration.

6.6.2 Cost Estimation

The migration comprises several steps. If the decision has already been made to deactivate the old solution, you can also migrate the queries because the effort involved is not excessive. Even in extreme cases, it will never take more than 30 minutes at most to migrate a query, including a test phase and the conversion of the exceptions. You should allow an average of 10 to 15 minutes per query, which means that you can migrate and test between 30 and 50 queries in one day.

Query views are not migrated because you will continue to use the old views. When they are saved again, a 7.0 version is stored in the database in addition to the 3.5 version, which means that query views are both downward- and upward compatible. You don't need to allocate any time for this.

This isn't the case with the migration of web templates, however. As you've seen, it takes a lot of time to migrate even the simplest web template, in particular if you don't know how to convert certain constructs in the new release. When you are scheduling the migration of web templates, you must therefore include time for researching the new constructs that you'll have to use.

In exceptional cases, you may be lucky, and the migration may be virtually automatic from start to finish. This is the case if you haven't used any ABAP programs, a table interface, JavaScript, or SAP BW commands. In this scenario, you only need to invest time in the optical migration, which may also be completed in a relatively short space of time. This really is the exception because web templates are normally used to extract more information from a report.

If you are dealing with an exceptional case and therefore don't need to make any modifications in the form of the constructs specified previously, it may only take 15 to 30 minutes to complete the migration of a web template, including testing and visual adjustment. In other extreme cases, it may take several days to migrate a web template (in particular if functions are lost and this must be approved by the business department).

You should draw up an inventory of queries, query views, and web templates before the migration, and you should use categories to classify the web templates (e.g., 1 to 5, or simple to complex). Next, perform a test migration for a web template from each category, and record the time required in each case. This will give you a relatively accurate estimation of the time required for the complete migration. Figure 6.32 shows an example of how this document may appear.

Preparation for cost estimation

Web Templates

Techn. name	Description	Category
ZJWRS_T01	Top10 customers	2
ZJWRS_T02	Total view of suppliers	4
ZJWRS_T03	Information on suppliers	1
ZJWRS_T04	Personnel cost per personnel department	2
ZJWRS_T05	Illness rate per organizational unit	5
ZJWRS_T06	Analysis of absenteeism	3
ZJWRS_T07	Inventory	5
ZJWRS_T08	Number of entrances and leavings	3
ZJWRS_T09	Personnel head count (course of one year)	3
ZJWRS_T10	Personnel head count and FTE	2

Category	Effort	No. of reports	Total effort
1	1.5 hrs	1	1.5 hrs
2	3.5 hrs	3	10.5 hrs
3	5.0 hrs	3	15.0 hrs
4	8.0 hrs	1	8.0 hrs
5	12.0 hrs	2	24.0 hrs
Total		10	59.0 hrs

Figure 6.32 Preparation for Cost Estimation in Excel

A lot of time may also be saved if many of the web templates you've used are similar. Take this into account when estimating the time required for the relevant category. Remember to allow time for becoming familiar with the process and for testing. This will give you an accurate estimate based on your experience and expertise.

6.7 Summary

This chapter discussed the migration of web reporting. We began with a bird's eye view of how reporting works in SAP BW 3.5 and SAP NetWeaver BI and the key concepts in reporting: queries, query views, web templates, and reports. The query is the cornerstone of reporting. Filters and drilldowns can be saved globally in a query view called initial drilldown. You can create web templates (web applications) to modify the layout of a query. A report allows you to adapt to various output formats.

You then saw how each of these objects can be migrated. A query is usually migrated automatically. Query views don't need to be migrated, unlike web templates, which make up the lion's share of the migration. Reports are only available as of SAP NetWeaver BI and are therefore not relevant for migration.

We then migrated a sample query, and you saw how minor manual adjustments may also be required, for example, if exceptions were used.

Most of this chapter is dedicated to the subject of web template migration. You learned how to use the migration tool and which manual adjustments are required to complete a migration. You also saw how an optical migration (i.e., a modification of the layout) is necessary.

In the new SAP NetWeaver BI release, certain functions have unfortunately been discontinued or have been moved to the portal. As a result, it's more difficult or impossible to use these functions (e.g., the table interface). As a result, the effort involved in migration may be greater than you originally estimated.

We gave you four recommendations for performing a migration, which are recapped here:

1. **Necessity of the migration**
   Before you begin, make sure that the migration is really necessary.
2. **Query migration**
   As a rule, queries should not be migrated.
3. **Migration of web templates**
   Check each individual web template to determine whether it needs to be migrated.

4. **Migration of the reporting area**
   After a decision has been made in favor of a migration, perform a test migration of a number of simple reports and put together a valid cost estimation in consultation with the business department.

Lastly, you learned how to produce a relatively accurate estimate of the cost of migration (in terms of time and effort) based on your experience and expertise.

Appendices

A Bibliography

SAP AG, "Document Management in Knowledge Management," *http://help.sap.com/saphelp_nw70/helpdata/de/60/1c143bfaed272de10000000a11402f/content.htm.*

SAP AG, "SAP NetWeaver Upgrade Master," *https://service.sap.com/instguidesNW07* (Guide [S-User-ID] required).

Roland Kramer, "SAP NetWeaver 7.0 BI. Upgrade Specifics" (2007), *https://www.sdn.sap.com/irj/sdn/go/portal/prtroot/docs/library/uuid/10564d5c-cf00-2a10-7b87-c94e38267742.*

Horst Keller, and Sascha Krüger, *ABAP Objects* (Bonn: SAP PRESS, 2006).

SAP AG, "Using SAP BW Commands," *http://help.sap.com/saphelp_nw70/helpdata/de/71/8a784226d1d242e10000000a1550b0/content.htm.*

SAP AG, "SAP's Release Strategy" (2006), *http://www.sap.de/.*

SAP AG, "New SAP NetWeaver BI Capabilities in SAP NetWeaver 2004s," (SAP TechEd 2005).

SAP AG, "A Complete Look at Security for SAP NetWeaver BI," (SAP TechEd 2007).

B List of Acronyms

ABAP	Advanced Business Application Programming
API	Application Programming Interface
BEx	Business Explorer
BI	Business Intelligence
BIAC	BI Administration Cockpit
BW	Business Warehouse
CSS	Cascading Stylesheets
CSV	Comma Separated Values
DSO	DataStore Object
DTP	Data Transfer Process
EP	Enterprise Portal
ERP	Enterprise Resource Planning
ETL	Extraction Transformation Loading
FTE	Full Time Equivalent
GUI	Graphical User Interface
HCM	Human Capital Management
HR	Human Resources
HTML	Hypertext Markup Language
HTTP	Hypertext Transfer Protocol
HTTPS	Hypertext Transfer Protocol Secure
KM	Knowledge Management
ODS	Operational DataStore
OLAP	Online Analytical Processing
OLTP	Online Transactional Processing
OSS	Online Service System
PDF	Portable Document Format
PSA	Persistent Staging Area
RDA	Real-Time Data Acquisition

SAPI	Service API
SDN	SAP Developer Network
SLD	System Landscape Directory
SPS	Support Package Stack
SWDC	Software Distribution Center
URL	Uniform Resource Locator
WAD	Web Application Designer
WAS	Web Application Server
XHTML	Extended Hypertext Markup Language
XML	Extensible Markup Language

C Glossary

Analysis authorization In SAP NetWeaver BI, the analysis authorization enables you to map authorizations to reporting data. Because this authorization is no longer based on the SAP authorization object, it differs substantially from its predecessor, the reporting authorization. You can maintain analysis authorizations using Transaction RSECADMIN.

Authorization object Authorization objects are responsible for assigning authorizations in the SAP system. In the classic scenario, an authorization object is integrated into roles that are assigned to users.

DataSource In SAP BW and SAP NetWeaver BI, DataSources are used to extract data from a source system. A DataSource represents a conglomeration of fields that are extracted from the source system using different methods.

Data transfer process Data transfer processes serve to update data into data targets. They were introduced for the first time in SAP NetWeaver BI. Data transfer processes always connect persistent objects and are thus involved in each transformation. Compared to the InfoPackage used in SAP BW, the error-handling feature of data transfer processes has been improved.

Data target See InfoProvider

DSO object The DSO object (DataStore object) in SAP NetWeaver BI replaces the ODS object (Operational DataStore) used in SAP BW. It's used to store detail and transactional data.

ETL process ETL stands for Extraction Transformation Loading and describes the loading process from a source system through to the multidimensional structures (InfoCubes) of a data warehouse. The extraction process involves the actual data request, the transformation process cleanses and consolidates the incoming data, and loading refers to the final process of updating the data in the multidimensional data containers.

Field symbol Field symbols can be compared to pointers in the C programming language. A field symbol is used to dynamically access the contents of variables. Field symbols represent an advanced technique in ABAP development.

InfoCube An InfoCube is a multidimensional object that's structured according to the extended star schema of SAP. InfoCubes can contain data from different source systems for reporting purposes. An InfoCube may consist of a maximum of 16 dimensions and 255 key figures, with dimensions and key figures being mapped as InfoObjects.

InfoObject InfoObjects represent the smallest entity to contain data. An InfoObject can either have the type characteristic or key figure.

InfoPackage In SAP BW, InfoPackages are used to request data from a source system and to update this data in data targets. In SAP NetWeaver BI, in turn, InfoPackages are only responsible for requesting data, whereas the data update is carried out by a data transfer process.

InfoProvider InfoProviders represent objects in an SAP NetWeaver BI system on which you can define a query. These objects include the following:

- DataStore object (DSO)
- InfoCube
- InfoObject
- VirtualProvider
- InfoSet
- MultiProvider

The first three of these objects are also referred to as data targets because they contain physical data. The last three objects in the preceding list are merely logical views to datasets and do not contain any physical data.

Information Broadcaster The Information Broadcaster is a tool that enables you to precalculate, schedule, and dispatch reports. In SAP BW, the Information Broadcaster was integrated via a specific web item, whereas in SAP NetWeaver BI, it's stored centrally in SAP NetWeaver Portal.

InfoSource In SAP BW, InfoSources are mandatory objects within the data flow from a DataSource to the InfoProviders. An InfoSource does not contain any physical data and is used for the transformation from source fields to target fields. In SAP NetWeaver BI, InfoSources are optional.

ODS object In an SAP BW system, ODS objects (Operational DataStore) are used to store transactional detail data. In SAP NetWeaver BI, this type of object was replaced by the DSO object, which has the same function.

PSA The PSA (persistent staging area) is used for the initial storage of data during a data request process from source systems. The InfoPackage requests the data and stores it in the PSA before it is updated further.

Query To analyze the dataset in an SAP NetWeaver BI system, you generally need a query as a basis. A query represents a request to an InfoProvider, which is created using the SAP BEx Query Designer.

Query View Within a query, you can capture and save individual views. This way, you can make sure that the query has the same layout as before the next time you call it, for example, with a deactivated hierarchy and sorted by a specific key figure.

Real-time data acquisition (RDA) The real-time data acquisition extracts data from an SAP source system in real time. As soon as a source system contains new data, this data is recognized and extracted into the SAP NetWeaver BI system.

Reporting Agent The Reporting Agent enables you to precalculate reports and is an integral component of the Administrator Workbench (RSA1) in SAP BW. It is no longer available in SAP NetWeaver BI because its functionality is now provided by the Information Broadcaster.

Reporting authorization The reporting authorization is used in SAP BW to map authorizations to reporting data. Because it's based on the SAP authorization object, it differs substantially from its successor, the analysis authorization. You can maintain reporting authorizations using Transaction RSSM.

Sandbox system A sandbox system represents a kind of test system that's used for the technical migration process. You set up a sandbox system to "practice" the migration process in a sample system using live data. After the migration has finished, the sandbox system is usually de-installed again.

SAP Business Explorer Suite The SAP Business Explorer Suite, or Business Explorer (BEx) for short, consists of reporting applications for SAP NetWeaver BI. These applications allow you to create queries to the multidimensional dataset in the data warehouse. The Business Explorer Suite consists of the following applications:

- BEx Query Designer
- BEx Analyzer
- BEx Web Application Designer
- BEx Report Designer (new in SAP NetWeaver BI)

Transfer rule In SAP BW, the transfer rule is used to transfer data from a DataSource to an InfoSource. In SAP NetWeaver BI, the transfer rule was replaced by the transformation.

Transformation In SAP NetWeaver BI, the transformation replaces the transfer and update rules that are used in SAP BW. It is used to transform source fields into target fields and provides a higher degree of flexibility in the update process.

Update rule Update rules are used to update data from an InfoSource or InfoProvider into an InfoProvider in SAP BW. In SAP NetWeaver BI, the transformation has replaced the update rule.

Web application A web application is an object from reporting that is used to create custom query designs. You can create web applications, which are often referred to as web templates, using the BEx Web Application Designer.

Web item The Web Application Designer enables you to create your own web templates, which, in turn, allow you to display queries. Basic elements — the so-called web items — are responsible for the display. Web items include tables, graphics, filters, and selection boxes.

Web template See Web application

D Translation of Web Items

This section contains translations of web items that differ in Releases SAP Web Application Designer 3.5 and 7.0. Web items that are no longer available are marked as "deleted"; new web items are marked as "not available" in the WAD 3.5 column.

Web Item (WAD 3.5)	Web Item (WAD 7.0)
ABC classification	deleted
Ad-hoc Query Designer	deleted
Alert Monitor	deleted
Broadcaster	deleted
Chart	Chart
Checkboxes	Checkbox Group
Dropdown Box	Dropdown Box
Filter	Info Field
Hierarchical Filter Selection	Hierarchical Filter Selection
Map	Map
Key Figure Overview	deleted
Label	Text
Navigation Block	Navigation Area
not available	Container Layout
not available	Filter Area
not available	Menu Bar
not available	Property Area
not available	Tabs
not available	Button Group
not available	Link
not available	Group
not available	Input Field

Table D.1 Translations of Web Items from WAD 3.5 to WAD 7.0

Web Item (WAD 3.5)	Web Item (WAD 7.0)
not available	System Messages
not available	Listbox
not available	Report
not available	Script
not available	Custom Extension (as of SPS 14)
Radio Button Group	Radio Button Group
Role Menu	deleted
Prediction Simulation	deleted
Table	Analysis
Text Elements	Info Field

Table D.1 Translations of Web Items from WAD 3.5 to WAD 7.0 (Cont.)

E Author

Daniel Knapp finished his studies of information technology at the Technical University of Ilmenau, Germany, in 2004. After that, he joined IXULT AG in Rosenheim, Germany, where he worked as an SAP Technology Consultant. Since 2006, he has been responsible for the Business Intelligence area at IT2 Solutions AG. His area of responsibility comprises the design and implementation of complex data models, the extraction of data from SAP and non-SAP systems, as well as the areas of reporting, analysis, and performance optimization in existing SAP business intelligence solutions.

In addition to implementing the SAP Business Information Warehouse/SAP NetWeaver Business Intelligence his work also focuses on integrating the NetWeaver Portal in the Human Capital Management (HCM) environment and on implementing Employee and Manager Self-Services. He has released several publications and given speeches at trade fairs and congresses on the topic of business intelligence.

Daniel Knapp is the author of several SAP PRESS books, including *Developing SAP Applications with Adobe Flex* (2006), which he co-authored with Armin Lorenz, Gunther Schöppe, Felix Consbruch, and Frank Sonnenberg; *HR with SAP NetWeaver Portal* (2007, available only in German under the title *Personalwirtschaft mit SAP NetWeaver Portal*), which he co-authored with Harald Goetsch and Sven Herrmann; and Practical Data Modeling for SAP NetWeaver BI (2008, currently available only in German under the title "Praktische Datenmodellierung für SAP NetWeaver BI").

Index

L

M

N

O

P

Q

R

V

W

X

ISBN 978-1-59229-228-8

1st Edition 2009

German Edition first published 2008 by Galileo Press, Bonn, Germany.

Galileo Press is named after the Italian physicist, mathematician and philosopher Galileo Galilei (1564–1642). He is known as one of the founders of modern science and an advocate of our contemporary, heliocentric worldview. His words *Eppur si muove* (And yet it moves) have become legendary. The Galileo Press logo depicts Jupiter orbited by the four Galilean moons, which were discovered by Galileo in 1610.

Editor Eva Tripp
English Edition Editor Jon Franke
Translation Lemoine International, Inc., Salt Lake City, UT
Copy Editor Julie McNamee
Cover Design Silke Braun
Cover Image Getty Images/Krzysztof Dydynski
Layout Design Vera Brauner
Production Kelly O'Callaghan
Typesetting Publishers' Design and Production Services, Inc.
Printed and bound in Canada